THE BRIGHT SIDE OF BROKENNESS

...

What Broke You Has Also Built You

LARRY KOOYMAN

CONTENTS

DEDICATION

For Momma

You left this world in November 2024, and not a day passes
that I don't feel the space where you used to be.

You were imperfect and brave and human and mine.

You fought battles I couldn't fully see, and you loved me
the best way you knew how.

That was enough. You were enough.

"I love you bunches."

Always.

To My Bride

Without your love and your steadiness, none of this would exist.

You see me fully ... every scar, every shadow,
every unfinished piece ... and you stay.

Because of you, I believe I can reach for things that
used to feel too far away.

My heart is yours. It has been for a long time,
and it will be long after these pages are read.

Building this life with you and for our children is the
greatest work I've ever done.

To JD & Cali

If you are reading this as the children you are right now ...
I love you more than this page can hold.

If you are reading this as the adults I already know you will become ... I
hope you can hear my voice in these words.

I wrote this book so that the pain I carried would not be wasted.
But I also wrote it for you. So that one day, when life hands you
something heavy, you will know that your dad carried heavy things too
... and found a way through. And so will you.

You were both born into something different than what I had.
Your mom and I made sure of that. Not because we are perfect parents
... we are not. But because we love you with the kind of love that
chooses, every single day, to do better than what came before.

You are rooted. Deeply, fully, permanently rooted in love.

There is nothing you could do, nowhere you could go,
no version of yourself you could become that would ever
change the way I feel about you.

I am proud of you today. I will be proud of you tomorrow.
I was proud of you before you ever did a single thing to earn it.

Your mom believes in you with everything she has. So do I.

Whatever storms come ... and some will ...
you will not face them alone.

My heart is always with you. Both of you. Always.

I love you bunches.

PREFACE

The Night the Answer Found Me

I didn't plan to write this book.

I'm not sure you can plan something like this. Some things have to find you first.

Dani and I have a ritual. Most evenings, after the noise of the day settles, we sit together and just... talk. About life. About dreams. About where we've been and where we're headed. We call it Date Night, and it's one of the most important things we do.

That particular night, I was in a familiar struggle. The past had followed me into the room again, the way it tends to do when the house gets quiet. I was carrying the weight of old questions I'd never fully answered. The ones that start with why.

Dani was scrolling through her phone and paused. A friend of ours out in the Reno area had posted something. They were walking through real loss... the kind that hollows you out slowly. And in their post, they mentioned something that stopped Dani mid-scroll.

They had found comfort in a story. Specifically, in a film that a good friend of ours here in Nashville had made about their own life experience. This person had taken the hardest parts of what they'd lived through and turned it into something people could watch, feel, and carry with them.

And our friend in Reno, deep in their grief, had watched it... and found solid ground. A handhold. The quiet but unmistakable relief of realizing,

"Someone else has been here. I'm not alone in this."

Dani read it to me out loud.

One person's pain had become another person's lifeline.

And something cracked open in me.

Because I have spent a significant portion of my life wrestling with a question I could never fully silence. A question that surfaces in the dark, in the quiet moments between everything else:

Why, God? Why did You let all of that happen to me?

I've asked it with anger. I've asked it with tears. I've asked it in the middle of success when, by every external measure, I had no right to still be haunted by it.

I've never fully stopped asking it.

But that night, sitting in our living room while Dani read those words to me... something shifted. I felt it physically. Like a pressure in my chest that had been there so long I'd forgotten it wasn't normal.

And in that moment, as clear and calm as I've ever heard anything in my life, I felt God's presence settle over me. Not loud. Not dramatic. Just...present. The way a hand feels when it rests on your shoulder and you know, without turning around, exactly who it is.

"That's why I let you go through all of that. So you can tell your story."

That was the answer.

Not a justification. Not a theological argument. Just a quiet, weighty, unmistakable answer to the question I'd carried for decades.

Your pain may not be for you.

It may be for the person sitting in Reno. Or the one in the parking lot of a church, afraid to walk inside. Or the kid who grew up in a house that looked fine from the outside but sounded like a war zone from the inside. Or the adult version of that kid, who has never heard anyone say out loud the things they've only dared to think.

Your story...the one you've been ashamed of, the one you've edited and buried and minimized...might be the exact map someone else desperately needs.

That's the epiphany that built this book.

And like anyone who hears a clear call toward obedience...I'm answering it.

Who I Am and Why I Can Speak to This

I am not a therapist. I'm not a pastor or a clinical researcher.

I am a husband, a father, a martial arts school owner, and a leadership developer. I've spent the better part of my adult life helping people discover what they're made of...kids on the mat learning discipline and confidence, school owners learning to build businesses with purpose, leaders learning to lead from the inside out.

My credentials for this book aren't on a wall. They're in the chapters ahead.

I was two years old the first time I saw my mother's blood.

I was three when I watched my father press a gun to her temple.

I was a teenager watching my mother go through detox... again... hoping this time would be the time it finally stuck.

And I was an adult when I finally had to pack my own bags and walk away from the house I'd been trying to save...because staying was costing me everything I'd worked to become.

I know what it's like to grow up in a storm you didn't create.

I know what it's like to be handed counterfeit love and told to be grateful for it.

I know what it's like to carry a childhood like a stone in your chest through your twenties, your thirties, your marriage, your business, your best days.

And I know...because I've lived it...what it looks like when the chain finally breaks.

That's why I'm qualified to write this. Not because I have all the answers. But because I've been deep enough inside the questions to know the way out.

What This Book Is...and What It Is Not

This is not a book about shame.

Enough of that has already been had. Carried. Worn. Passed around like something that belongs to no one and somehow ends up with everyone.

This is not a book designed to generate sympathy or cast judgment on the people in these pages. The people in my story were broken in their own ways, shaped by their own storms, fighting battles I could only partially see. I am not writing this to expose them. I am writing it to expose the patterns...so we can finally stop repeating them.

What this book is: a conversation between someone who walked through darkness and someone who might be standing at the edge of it right now.

In these chapters, you will find stories from my life. Real ones. The kind with sharp edges. I'll share the details not to shock you, but because sanitized stories don't save anyone. The truth has to be specific enough to recognize. If you've lived something like this, you'll know it when you read it...and you'll know you're not alone.

Each chapter is built around a real memory. A moment that could have defined me by what it took. Instead, I want to show you what each one gave...the lesson buried inside the loss, the clarity carved out of the chaos.

Because there is a bright side to brokenness.

Not a silver lining that dismisses the pain.

Not toxic positivity dressed up in a bow.

A genuine, hard-won, scar-tested truth:

What broke you has also built you. And what built you can now build someone else.

A Word Before We Begin

If you picked up this book because you're carrying something heavy...welcome. You're in the right place.

If you picked it up because someone you love is struggling and you want to understand...this is for you, too.

If you're a parent, a leader, a survivor trying to make sense of what happened and figure out what comes next...keep reading.

I was obedient to the call to tell this story. What you do with it is between you and God.

But my prayer is simple:

That somewhere in these pages, you find the same thing our friend found that night...solid ground, a handhold, and the quiet certainty that someone else has been here.

And made it through.

With everything I have,

Larry Kooyman

CHAPTER ONE

INHERITED STORMS AREN'T YOUR FAULT

I don't remember falling asleep.

I just remember being awake.

That's how it always started. No transition, no warning. One moment there was nothing... the thick, unconscious dark of an infant's sleep... and then suddenly there was everything. Sound. Fear. The kind of alert that bypasses every cognitive layer and goes straight to the body.

I was still in my crib. The kind with the dropdown rail on the side... you'd unlatch it and the front panel would swing down so you could lift the child in and out. I remember that crib more clearly than I should at that age. The feel of the rails under my hands. The way the mattress sat just high enough that I could pull myself up to standing and grip the top rail and look out. I did that a lot, apparently. My mother used to say I always woke up standing, never lying down. Like even in sleep some part of me was ready to move.

I was eighteen months old. Maybe two years. I couldn't tell you with certainty and neither could the adults in my life by the time I was old enough to ask. Time is strange that way... the things that matter most to a child are often the things adults are least precise about.

What I know is this: I was small enough to still be in a crib. And I was old enough to remember.

Both of those things matter.

The Sound Before the Silence

It started as voices.

Not the ordinary backdrop noise of parents existing in the same small space... the murmur of television, the slide of cabinet doors, water running. This was different. The pitch was wrong. The frequency was wrong. Even at eighteen months, before I had language for what I was hearing, I had a body that understood threat. And my body understood this immediately.

The voices were escalating.

My father's, low and hard-edged. My mother's, climbing toward something I can only describe as desperation... not just anger, not just frustration, but the sound of a person who has been here before and knows what comes next and is trying, with everything she has, to stop it.

I stood at the crib rail and held on.

We lived in a trailer. Single-wide. The walls were thin in the way that trailer walls always are... you could hear conversations in normal tones through them, let alone this. Let alone screaming. There was no distance between me and what was happening in that room. No buffer. No insulation of space or architecture that might have softened the edges of it.

I was maybe fifteen feet from the worst thing I would ever witness.

The screaming grew. And I want to be careful here... careful to describe this accurately, because there is a specific kind of screaming that I've never heard replicated in film or television or any manufactured version of fear. What I heard that night was the sound of a human being reaching the absolute end of what they can endure. Not rage in the theatrical sense. Not the kind of volume that's trying to make a point. This was the sound of something escaping from a place so deep inside a person that it couldn't be contained anymore. The anguish was larger than the body trying to hold it.

My mother screamed like that.

And then came the crack.

One sound, flat and sharp, like the single snap of something breaking. It stopped me cold. I gripped the rail tighter. I didn't breathe.

And then it came again.

And again.

My father's hand against my mother's body. I didn't understand the mechanics of it then. I just understood the sound. And the sound told me something that no child should ever have confirmed at that age: that one person could choose to hurt another. That the choice could be made deliberately. Repeatedly. Without stopping.

I don't know how long it lasted. Time doesn't work right under conditions like that. Fear compresses and expands it in ways that make accurate recollection impossible. What I know is that it lasted long enough that it became a sound I would carry in my body for years... something that lived below conscious memory, that would surface in unexpected places, triggered by nothing and everything.

And then it stopped.

The silence that followed was not peaceful. It was the kind of silence that arrives after catastrophe... after the tornado passes and you climb out of the cellar and the world looks completely different than it did. That kind of silence. The kind that says: whatever was here before is gone now.

I stood at the rail and I waited.

I waited for my mother's voice. For any sound that would tell me she was still there. That whatever had just happened hadn't taken her somewhere I couldn't follow.

Nothing.

The silence held.

And in that silence, I made a decision.

The Climb

I have thought about this moment many times over the years. The moment I decided to climb out of that crib and walk toward the thing I was afraid of.

I wasn't brave. I want to be clear about that. I wasn't some unusually courageous child operating beyond my developmental stage. I was terrified. My heart was going fast the way a child's heart goes fast... the kind of fear that is physical before it is anything else. My legs were probably shaking. My hands were probably shaking.

But my mother had gone quiet. And I needed to know why.

That need... the need to find her, to confirm she was still there... was stronger than the fear. That's not courage. That's love. And love at eighteen months is not philosophical or reasoned. It's raw. It's the most unfiltered form of it there is. You need the person. You go find them.

I swung one leg over the rail. Felt for the edge with my foot. The drop was significant from my perspective... probably three and a half feet to the floor, which at that size might as well have been ten. I held on as long as I could, arms stretched to their limit, and then let go.

The floor hit my feet hard.

Cold. The floor was cold. I remember that detail with absolute clarity... the shock of it, the way it jolted me fully awake, fully present. The floor of that trailer at whatever hour this was, on whatever season night it was, was cold linoleum and it grounded me immediately into the reality of where I was and what I was doing.

I stood there for a moment. Listened.

Still nothing from their room.

I walked to my bedroom door and stepped into the hallway.

The hallway... and I use that word generously for what it actually was... was a narrow corridor of dark. But at the far end, coming from beneath their door, was an orange glow. Not bright. Not the hard fluorescent light of a bathroom or the warm lamp-light of a bedroom being used normally. This was the dimmer, amber kind of glow that suggested a single overhead bulb, or possibly a lamp with the shade askew. It was the color of something that had been running too long. That needed rest.

The door was cracked. Not much... maybe an inch. Not enough to see through. But enough that light escaped around the edges and the smell reached me before I got close.

Cigarette smoke, first. That I recognized. It was part of the atmosphere of that house, a constant low-grade background note. The furniture held it. The curtains held it. It wasn't alarming on its own.

And underneath it, stale beer. Flat. The kind of smell that had been open for hours and settled into the room.

I put my hand on the door and pushed it open.

The hinge creaked. Those old hollow-core interior doors with the cheap plastic lever handles... they always creaked at the hinge, a high, thin sound that felt enormous in that silence. I remember thinking, even then, that the sound was too loud. That it would change things.

It did.

Some Doors Can't Be Unopened

My mother was on the floor beside the bed.

Not sitting. Not leaning. Slumped... the specific posture of someone whose body has used all of its reserves. Her back was against the side of the mattress, her legs extended out onto the floor in front of her, and her hands were covering her face. Both hands, pressed flat against her cheeks and forehead. Her shoulders were moving. She was crying... not loudly anymore, but in that deep, internal way where the sound is mostly breath. Shuddering exhales. The aftermath of sobbing.

Her hair was down and disheveled. I remember the makeup... dark lines running down her face from beneath her hands where the mascara had tracked her tears. I remember that detail with unusual clarity, probably because it was the first time I'd ever seen her face look wrong. She was always put together in the way that young mothers of that era were. Hair done. Makeup on. Even in that small trailer, she had maintained something... some version of dignity or presentation that the circumstances around her constantly worked to erode.

This was what happened when the erosion won.

Her eyes were swollen. Not from the violence... or not only from that. From the crying. From the quantity of tears that had passed through them. The skin around them was puffy and red in a way that takes a long time to develop. This hadn't just started.

My father was on the other side of the room.

His back was toward me. He registered the door opening... I know this because his head moved slightly, a fractional turn of the shoulder that told me he'd heard the creak and knew I was there. He didn't look at me directly. Didn't turn around. Didn't cross the room. Didn't say anything.

Instead, I heard the flick of a Zippo lighter.

That sound. Metal on metal, the snap of the lid, the scrape of the wheel, the soft whomp of the flame catching. He lit a cigarette. In the silence following everything that had just happened in that room, with his child standing in the doorway and his wife broken on the floor... he lit a cigarette.

I still hear that sound. A Zippo lighter anywhere... a movie, a crowded street, someone at the next table at a restaurant... and something in me tightens. The body doesn't forget. It keeps the record long after the mind would prefer to let it go.

He dismissed me without a word.

I want you to hold that for a moment. Because it is one of the most clarifying details of my entire childhood. Not the violence... though that is damning enough. But this: a man who heard his infant child come through a door in the middle of the night, after what had just happened in that room, and chose to turn away. Chose to light a cigarette. Chose absence over presence. Chose to be inconvenienced rather than moved.

There was no protective instinct. No shame. No pivoting toward the child who needed an adult to tell him things were okay... even if that would have been a lie.

Just a lighter. Just smoke. Just a back turned on two people who needed him.

I didn't look at him. I looked at her.

My mother's eyes found mine from behind her hands and I watched something move across her face... a sequence I've only understood much later. First: terror. The terror of a mother who realizes her child has seen this. Who in an instant understands that something has just been written into a small person that cannot be unwritten. The terror of permanent damage.

And then, immediately after: love.

The terror didn't go away... but love moved in front of it. She opened her arms.

I ran to her.

She pulled me in and held me with the particular tightness of someone who needs you as much as you need them. Her arms were shaking. She pressed my head against her chest and I could feel her heartbeat... fast, uneven, still working to slow itself down from whatever the body goes through when it's been through what hers had just been through.

And that's when I smelled it.

Not in the hallway. Not at the door. Here. In her arms. That close.

Iron. Metal. Salt.

Blood has a smell that most people never have to learn. It's dense and metallic, something you feel in the back of the throat more than the nose. Mixed with the beer and cigarette smoke already in that room, it became something else entirely... something layered and specific and unlike anything I'd encountered before.

I've caught it over the years in the most unexpected places. Walking past a bar on a summer night. A stranger passing on the street carrying the wrong combination of things. Cheap beer and smoke and that metallic undercurrent. When those three things arrive together, I'm immediately back in that room. Pressed against my mother. Eighteen months old. Feeling the drip of her tears on the back of my head, running warm down my neck.

She was broken. She was bleeding. She was the one who had just been hurt. And she was comforting me.

I didn't understand that then. I just needed her. I just held on.

Somewhere behind us, cigarette smoke drifted. The lighter had done its job. My father existed in that room like furniture... present, indifferent, taking up space without contributing anything to it.

I kept my face buried in her.

She smelled like everything that was happening... beer, smoke, copper, salt... but underneath all of it she still smelled like my mother. And that smell was the only thing in that moment that told me things might somehow be okay.

They weren't. Not for a long time.

But something else happened in that moment too. Something I didn't have words for then and have only understood slowly over the years.

I made a vow.

Not in language. Not in anything a two-year-old could articulate. But something in me... some part that was already watching, already recording, already beginning to form a self out of the raw material of these experiences... made a decision.

I will never be the reason someone looks like this.

I will never cause this.

I didn't know yet what I would do with that resolve. I didn't know how far away a different life was, or how many more nights like this one would come before anything changed. I didn't know that the years ahead would test that vow in ways I couldn't imagine.

But the vow was made.

And vows made in moments like that... they hold.

· · ·

What Gets Deposited

I've spent a lot of years thinking about memory. About what it keeps and what it releases and why.

Most of childhood is a blur. Not because nothing happened... plenty happened... but because the brain doesn't prioritize the unremarkable. The ordinary days dissolve. The routines dissolve. The afternoons and the dinners and the background texture of a life... most of it goes.

But the charged moments stay. The moments where emotion runs high... where fear or love or grief or wonder are present in full force... those get encoded differently. The brain treats them as important. It holds onto them.

Which means that for many of us who grew up inside dysfunction, our earliest and clearest memories are the worst ones. The fights. The fear. The nights we should never have witnessed. While the ordinary, safe, unremarkable moments... the ones that might have balanced the record... dissolve.

That's not a design flaw. That's just how memory works under pressure.

But it creates a problem. Because if the clearest things you can remember from childhood are the frightening things, you begin... without realizing it... to build your identity around them. Not around the whole truth of who you were or who you could become. Around the worst moments you survived.

And the worst moments have a way of whispering things.

As I grew older and the violence continued, I started to notice patterns I was too young to understand but old enough to absorb. My father's anger was often connected to my mother's attention toward me. The way she looked at me. The way she held me. The way, when I was in the room, her focus shifted.

In the broken logic of an abusive mind, love has to be competed for. Someone's gain is someone else's loss. My mother loving me was, to my father, something being taken from him. And the violence was, in part, his response to that.

I didn't understand any of that then. What I understood was consequence. Cause and effect in the rawest form. I existed. Bad things happened. The timeline was consistent.

The math a small child does with that information is devastating.

What if this is because of me?

What if my being here is the problem?

Those questions don't announce themselves as distorted thinking. They feel like logic. They feel like the reasonable conclusion of available evidence. A child doesn't have the developmental capacity to recognize the manipulation embedded in an abusive dynamic. They just experience the outcomes and try to make sense of them with the tools they have.

And so guilt takes root.

Not loud guilt. Not guilt that announces itself. The quiet kind. The kind that lives underneath everything else and shapes how you move through the world without you realizing it's doing so. The kind that makes you apologize before you've done anything wrong. That makes you shrink in spaces where you have every right to take up room. That makes you work twice as hard to prove you deserve to be here, because some deep-down part of you absorbed the message that your presence was a problem.

That guilt is a liar.

And I want to be direct with you about that, because I spent years not knowing it was lying to me.

. . .

Generational Math

Here is something nobody told me until I was well into adulthood, and it changed everything when I finally understood it:

The storm wasn't built for you. It was built long before you.

My father didn't become who he was in a vacuum. He was shaped... bent, broken, distorted... by what was done to him before I was born. His father before him. Whatever came before that. I don't know the full history. I never will. But I know enough about how these patterns work to understand that nobody arrives at the behavior I witnessed in that trailer room without having had something done to them first.

That is not an excuse. I want to be very clear: understanding the origin of someone's damage does not excuse what they do with it. My father made choices. Choices have consequences. The fact that he was also a broken person does not erase what his brokenness cost my mother or what it deposited into me.

But understanding the origin does something else: it separates you from it.

When you understand that the dysfunction you were born into was already in motion... that it had momentum and history and roots that had nothing to do with you... you can begin to see yourself as something other than the cause. You can begin to see yourself as someone who was caught in something. Someone who survived something. Someone who, with the right information and the right work, can choose a different direction.

Generational trauma is real. It's documented. It travels through families not by magic but by mechanics... through modeling, through exposure, through the neural pathways that form in children who are raised inside chaos. We learn what we see. We repeat what we absorbed. We build relationships that feel familiar even when familiar is harmful.

Unless we interrupt it.

The interruption is what this book is about.

Not the trauma itself... though we'll look at it honestly, because you can't interrupt what you won't examine. But the interruption. The decision point. The moment when a person looks at the pattern they inherited and says: not further. Not through me. This stops here.

I've made that decision. It cost something. It required work I wasn't prepared for and conversations I didn't want to have and a level of self-examination that is genuinely uncomfortable at times.

But the alternative... to keep passing the storm forward... was something I decided at eighteen months old I would not do.

I just didn't know yet how to build the life that would make that vow real.

That's what I learned.

That's what I want to give you.

. . .

The Bright Side

The title of this book is not ironic.

I didn't call it The Bright Side of Brokenness to be clever or to minimize what pain actually costs. I called it that because I believe it... because I've lived long enough and dug deep enough to know that the broken places in a person's story are not disqualifiers. They are not evidence of permanent damage. They are, if you're willing to examine them with honesty and courage, some of the most important materials you have.

The night I walked through that door and saw my mother on the floor... that image has never left me. It never will. It is part of the architecture of who I am. But what that night also gave me, pressed into me at a cellular level, was a clarity about what I would not become. About what I would not allow to pass forward. About the kind of man, husband, and father I was determined to be.

Pain is a terrible teacher with an excellent track record.

What you carry from your hardest moments... if you carry it consciously, if you examine it rather than just endure it... can become the foundation of something genuinely different. Something better than what was handed to you.

Not in spite of the brokenness.

Because of it.

That's the bright side. 27

It doesn't erase the dark. But it means the dark wasn't wasted.

. . .

CHAPTER TWO

MANIPULATION ALWAYS LEAVES CASUALTIES

The night I walked through that door didn't end things.

It was just the first one I remember.

After that, I lost count.

Some nights were small. A raised voice that didn't go anywhere. A door that closed a little too hard. The kind of tension that fills a small space and makes everyone move carefully, like you're navigating a room where the floor might give. Those nights you'd hold your breath, and then nothing would happen, and you'd exhale and wonder if you'd imagined the whole thing.

Other nights were not small.

Other nights were the same nightmare. Different date on the calendar.

My mother tried to hide it. She was good at that... or she tried to be. She had a way of managing the visible, of keeping the surface of things intact even when everything underneath was falling apart. But bruises have given and withheld on a schedule designed to destabilize... the child doesn't fail.

The adult does.

The system does.

The person who designed the game does.

And the guilt that gets installed in you during that time... the guilt of having taken the candy, of having looked forward to the reward, of having been confused by the warmth and the violence living inside the same person... that guilt is not evidence of your complicity.

It is evidence that the manipulation worked.

Which means it is not guilt you need to carry.

It is understanding.

. . .

Don't Let the Game Change You

I want to say one more thing before we close this chapter. And I want to say it carefully, because it matters more than it might seem.

Learning to see manipulation clearly does not have to make you hard.

I am not jaded. I am not suspicious of every kind gesture or waiting for the catch on every gift. That is not what this is. What this is... is recognition. The board is familiar now. I know the pieces. I know the moves. And because I know them, I simply choose not to play.

their own timeline. They don't cooperate with the story you're trying to tell. And in a single-wide trailer in a small town, there's nowhere to hide that keeps the neighbors from noticing, nowhere to go that doesn't eventually require an explanation.

So she stayed home.

Kept the blinds down. Wore long sleeves. Said she wasn't feeling well.

Nobody came to check.

What Nobody Was Talking About

I need to stop here, before we go any further, and say something about the world this was happening inside of.

This was not a time when abuse was discussed. Not openly. Not honestly. It wasn't a topic that appeared in the news with any real weight, not something a woman could walk into a police station or a church or a doctor's office and say plainly and expect to be believed and helped.

This was a time when, if a woman showed up somewhere with the evidence of what had happened written on her face, the first question people asked... quietly, or sometimes not so quietly... was: what did she do to deserve it?

Read that again. Because it matters.

Not: who did this to her. Not: how do we help. But: what did she do.

The cultural logic of that era was not subtle. A woman's place was in the home. The man was the head of the household. Whatever happened inside the walls of a marriage was a private matter. And if a woman couldn't keep her husband happy... if dinner was late, if the house wasn't right, if she said the wrong thing at the wrong moment... well. That was on her.

She was expected to do better next time.

The weight of what was happening in our trailer was almost entirely my mother's to carry. Not because she had done anything wrong. Not because she deserved it. But because the world around her had decided, collectively and quietly, that this was how things worked. That a man's anger was something a woman managed. That leaving was failure. That speaking about it was worse than enduring it.

She was trapped inside the violence and inside the silence that surrounded it.

Both of those things were real. Both of them were heavy.

And nobody... not one person... was telling her that either one of them was wrong.

. . .

How He Snapped

He didn't need much of a reason. That was one of the first things I came to understand, though I had no words for it at the time.

Dinner not ready. The trailer not clean enough. A look she gave him that landed wrong. A tone she used that he decided meant something it didn't. The list of what could set him off was so long and so inconsistent that there was no preparing for it. No getting ahead of it. No being good enough to prevent it. The rules changed without announcement, and the penalty for breaking them was always the same.

I remember one night... I would have been two, maybe three. Old enough to have toys. Old enough to leave them out the way any toddler does, scattered across the floor in that particular chaos that means someone small has been playing and alive and happy in a space.

He didn't see childhood.

He saw disorder.

I remember the sound of his voice before anything else. That pitch. That register that bypassed language and went straight into the body. And then I remember watching him cross the room, grab my toy box... the whole thing... and lift it and flip it upside down. Everything hit the floor at once. Plastic and noise and scatter. And then he was standing over me, red-faced and enormous, yelling at me to pick it all up.

I was a toddler.

With toys on the floor.

And I was learning, in that moment, the same thing my mother had already learned: that his anger didn't need a real reason. That it just needed a direction. And on any given night, that direction could be anything.

Or anyone.

Those were the smaller nights.

The bigger ones followed the same shape. He'd get angry. He'd leave. He'd go to the bar... one of those places that exists in every small town, dim inside regardless of the hour, smelling of something sour and permanent. He'd sit there for a few hours. And then he'd come home. Still carrying it. Still aimed.

And we'd live through it again.

As a child, you absorb these rhythms without knowing you're absorbing them. You learn the pattern the way you learn anything early… not through study, but through repetition. Through your body knowing before your mind does. The sound of a vehicle pulling into the driveway. The way a door opened when he'd been drinking. The way the air in the trailer changed before a word was said.

I was three years old and I already knew the difference between a door that opens normally and a door that opens into danger.

Children are not supposed to know that difference.

. . .

What Came After

Here is the part I haven't said yet. The part that took me years to fully understand. The part that still lands heavy when I say it out loud.

After the fights… after the screaming, after whatever had just happened to my mother in that room… my father would come and get me.

Not to comfort me. Not because he felt guilty and wanted to make things right.

He'd pick me up, take me by the hand, buckle me into the van, and we'd drive off. Just the two of us. Into the night. Away from whatever was left of her on that floor.

He had a van. Not a truck… a van. Road-worn and carrying the particular smell of his life inside it. My seat was a milk crate… one of those plastic grated ones, the kind dairy deliveries used to come in. Set right between the two front seats. That was my spot. No seatbelt. No car seat. Just a small boy on a plastic crate, sitting up high enough to see out the windshield, close enough to feel the engine through the floorboards.

I loved that seat. I want to be honest about that, because it matters.

There was something about riding up front, being that close to him, the hum of the road at night with the darkness moving past the windows. It felt like being chosen. Like being the one he wanted with him. What I could not have understood then was what I was actually sitting next to. The smell of his breath in that van... I learned it before I had words for it. Not just beer. You could almost identify the brand by the weight and grain of it. Something flat and dense that years later I'd catch walking past a bar on a summer night and feel something tighten in my chest before I even knew why.

He was driving after drinking. With me on a milk crate between the seats.

And I thought it was the best seat in the house.

Sometimes we'd stop at a gas station. A dollar store. Wherever was open. And he'd tell me to pick something.

A toy. A candy. Whatever I wanted.

The candy I always picked was Necco Wafers.

The pastel colors. The way they dissolved on your tongue in a little burst of sweet and chalk. They were the kind of candy a kid asks for by name, the kind that felt like a specific treat rather than a generic one. He knew I loved them. And every time, there they were.

He'd hand them to me. He'd smile. He'd be warm and easy and attentive in a way he almost never was at home. And I... a toddler, a little kid who just needed his father to love him... would take the candy and hold it like it meant something.

Because to me, it did.

We'd drive around for a while. Sometimes he'd take me to the VFW hall, lift me up and set me right on the bar. I remember that place... the low ceilings, the amber warmth, the smell of stale beer and cigarettes and wood that had absorbed decades of both. And I remember him in that room. How different he was. A laugh that the room leaned toward. A way of talking that made people feel like the only one he was talking to. He'd put his hand on my shoulder and someone would say something about what a good-looking boy I was, and he'd grin like he'd built me himself.

Nobody in that bar saw what we lived with.

Nobody there would have believed it, probably.

That man... warm, charming, his kid on the bar beside him... that man didn't have anything to hide.

The monster came home. He left the charisma at the door.

We'd drive back eventually. He'd carry me inside. My mother would still be there... picking up whatever had shattered, trying to make the space calm again, trying to keep the next night from being like the last one. She'd look at me, then look away. The bag of candy and whatever toy he'd bought would land on the table like a receipt. Like evidence of something.

She knew exactly what that bag meant.

I did not.

. . .

What I Didn't Know I Was Learning

I'm going to tell you something that is hard to admit.

Genuinely hard. Even now.

I started to look forward to it.

Not the violence. I want to be precise about that, because precision matters here. I didn't look forward to what happened to my mother. I was a child, not a monster. But somewhere in the wiring of a three-year-old brain trying to make sense of an environment that made no sense at all, a pattern had formed. A sequence. A cause and effect so consistent that my nervous system had started treating it as reliable.

He would fight with her.

He would hurt her.

And then he would come get me.

And I would get the candy. And the van ride. And the warmth. And the version of my father that smiled at me and let me pick whatever I wanted and sat me up on a bar and put his hand on my shoulder like I was someone he was proud of.

That sequence repeated enough times that my nervous system began to connect the dots in the only direction available to it. The bad thing preceded the good thing. Consistently. Every time. And in a childhood that offered very little consistency about anything... that sequence, as terrible as the beginning of it was, became something my body recognized and waited for.

I didn't understand what I was being taught to expect.

I didn't understand that the gifts were tools.

That the candy was currency.

That my father was purchasing my presence and using it to send a message to my mother: see how much he loves me, see how he comes to me, see what you'll lose if you leave.

What I understood was that he took me with him. He chose me. He smiled at me over the hood of that van in a parking lot at midnight and let me pick the candy I wanted.

And for a little boy who had spent most of his waking hours watching his father hurt the person he loved most... that was oxygen.

I took it every time.

I looked forward to what made it possible.

Let that land for a moment. Because it needs to.

A toddler, conditioned by repetition and need and the particular desperation of a child who just wants his father to show up... had begun to associate his mother's suffering with something good coming for him.

That is not a character flaw.

That is what manipulation does to the people caught inside it.

. . .

The Weight I Carried Without Knowing Its Name

I've never gone to therapy. Not formally. Not the way I probably should have.

What I did instead was what a lot of people do. I internalized the memories and told myself they were handled. Packed them down somewhere below the surface. Locked them in the past and then lost the directions back. Figured if I kept moving forward... kept building, kept working, kept becoming someone different from what I'd come from... the weight would eventually stop mattering.

That is not how weight works.

I carried guilt for years. Not loud guilt. Not the kind that announces itself. The quiet kind that lives underneath everything else and shapes how you move through the world without you realizing it's doing the shaping. The kind that surfaces at strange moments. The kind that arrived, fully formed and immediate, any time I saw a roll of Necco Wafers.

Because at some point in my growing up, I understood what had actually been happening. I understood that while my mother lay on the floor of that trailer in a state of pure wreckage... her soul depleted, her body bruised, every reserve she had emptied out... my father had taken the one thing she was trying most desperately to protect. Me. And used it against her.

I was the leverage.

The candy was the transaction.

And I had participated. Eagerly. Joyfully. I had taken the candy with both hands and felt grateful. And... God help me... looked forward to the next time.

That understanding, when it finally arrived, landed hard.

I wish I had talked to someone sooner. I wish I had given myself permission to set that guilt down before I'd carried it so far. That's part of why I'm writing this. Because the years I spent dragging that weight before I understood what it actually was... those years cost something real.

But here is the other side of it.

The weight built something, too.

You don't develop the kind of clarity I have about manipulation... about the difference between a genuine gift and a transaction, about what it looks and feels like when love is used as leverage... you don't get that from reading about it. You get it from carrying it. From having it in your hands long enough to learn its specific texture.

Like working out. The weight is necessary to build the strength.

The weight I had to carry allows me to recognize the people still carrying their own.

I see you.

And I hope that somewhere in this story, you find the permission to set yours down.

. . .

What I've Chosen to Believe About Him

I've thought about this for a long time. Not with bitterness... or not only with that. But with the hard, genuine work of trying to understand something I may never fully understand.

Why did he take me out? Every time?

The answer I've landed on... the one that lives in the complicated space between compassion and honesty... is that maybe he needed to. Not just for control, though that was absolutely part of it. But because taking me with him, sitting me on that bar, watching people respond to his son and to him as a father... maybe that was the only place he could still feel like a decent man.

Maybe I was the evidence he needed that there was still something good in him.

That the monster he became inside that trailer wasn't the whole of what he was.

I'd like to think that. Genuinely. Not to excuse what he did. Not to minimize what it cost my mother, what it cost me, what it cost the version of our family that never got to exist. But because the alternative... a man who felt nothing, who had no internal contradiction, who was purely and entirely what those worst nights showed... that version doesn't leave room for the man who sat me on a bar and laughed with strangers and looked, for an hour, like someone's good father.

He was broken. Badly. In ways I can only see the shape of, not the full depth.

Broken people break things.

It does not excuse it. It does not balance the ledger.

But it is the most honest thing I have to offer about who he was.

. . .

What Manipulation Actually Is

Here is what I've come to understand about manipulation: it never announces itself.

It doesn't arrive with a sign around its neck. It doesn't feel like what it is. That is the entire point. If manipulation felt like manipulation, it wouldn't work. It works precisely because it disguises itself as something else. Generosity. Love. Care. The gift that says, see? It's not so bad. See how good I can be?

Abusers understand, on some level that may not even be fully conscious, that terror alone is unstable. That if all you ever do is take, the person you're taking from will eventually have nothing left to lose and will leave. So you give, too. Strategically. Just enough.

A night out. A candy. An apology that's just sincere-sounding enough to buy another week. A moment of warmth that makes the target wonder if maybe they're the problem. Maybe they provoked it. Maybe, if they could just get things right, he'd be like this all the time.

This is not love.

What was handed to me in those parking lots was not love. It looked like a treat. It functioned as a chain. And the cruelest part is that the chain wrapped around my mother far more tightly than it ever touched me. Because she had to watch her small son reach up and take the candy her abuser offered him and know... know with absolute clarity... that his happiness was being used as proof that everything was fine. As evidence that the man was not a monster. As the weight on the scale she'd have to tip every time she thought about leaving.

He's good with the boy. Look at how the boy loves him.

Maybe it's not that bad.

Manipulation always leaves casualties.

In our house, I was the collateral.

· · ·

You Are Not the Game

I'm telling you this because you may recognize something in it.

Maybe not Necco Wafers. Maybe not a VFW bar and a van and a milk crate and a toddler carried through the night. But the architecture of it. The way something was handed to you with strings attached that you couldn't see. The way someone used your love for them, or their love for you, or your need for their approval, as a tool to get what they wanted. The way you were made into a move in someone else's game without being told the rules, without being asked to play, without ever agreeing to any of it.

That is not your fault.

It was never your fault.

Children cannot consent to being weapons. They cannot protect themselves from adults who understand that love is leverage. All a child can do is love the people they need and hope that love is returned honestly. When it isn't... when the love is manufactured and deployed,

There is a difference between enlightenment and armor. Armor keeps everything out. Enlightenment lets you see what's coming and choose your response.

Don't let what was done to you make you callused. Don't let someone else's manipulation turn into your suspicion of everyone. Don't let the game convince you that everyone is playing it, because most people aren't. Most people are just trying to love well and be loved back.

What the game gave me... at a cost I would not wish on anyone... is the ability to tell the difference between real and counterfeit. Between a gift and a transaction. Between someone who is present because they want to be and someone who is present because they need something from you.

Let it enlighten you. Not harden you.

That is the only way the weight becomes worth what it cost.

. . .

The Bright Side

I still don't eat Necco Wafers.

I'm not sure I ever will.

But I don't hate them. And I don't hate the boy who ate them. And I don't hate my father... though that is its own chapter, and we will get there.

What I have is clarity. And clarity, it turns out, is one of the most useful things a person can carry forward from the places that hurt them most.

I am a husband now. A father. And I know with absolute certainty the difference between giving someone something because I love them and giving someone something because I need them to stay quiet, stay small, stay manageable.

The first one I practice every day.

The second one I refuse.

This is not your weight to bear.

Whatever guilt was installed in you by someone else's game... whatever shame you've been dragging that was never yours to carry... it was placed there by someone who needed you to hold it so they didn't have to.

You can put it down.

You are allowed to put it down.

You don't have to roll the dice. You don't have to play along. You don't have to be a piece on anyone's board.

The game ends the moment you recognize it for what it is.

And then... you walk away.

. . .

Chapter Three

What You Can't Un-See Becomes the Bridge

I've been sitting with this chapter longer than any other.

I've started it. Stopped. Walked away from it. Come back to it at odd hours when the house is quiet and the kids are asleep and I'm not sure why I'm even awake. I've written versions of it that circled the real thing without ever landing on it. Said the true version out loud to myself in empty rooms and not been able to follow it onto the page.

I don't fully know how to write these words.

I'm going to write them anyway.

Because I've carried this memory for most of my life. I've filed it. Buried it. Tried to shove it so deep that the light couldn't find it. I have told myself, more times than I can count, that it doesn't need to be touched. That it happened. That it's over. That revisiting it accomplishes nothing except ripping open something that finally, mercifully, went quiet.

But it never fully went quiet.

And I've finally started to understand why.

Some things are given to you not so you can keep them. But so you can eventually use them.

This is one of those things.

. . .

The Night

It started the same way the other nights started.

Voices. Then screaming. The particular escalation I already knew, even as a toddler, even before I had words for any of it. The same arguing. The same sounds of impact. The same soundtrack that had become, terribly, a kind of normal.

But something about this night was different.

Maybe it was the tone. Maybe it was louder than usual, or sharper, or carrying a frequency my small body had never quite registered before. I don't know how to explain it except to say that I was scared in a new way. Not the fear I already knew. Something underneath that. Something that felt less like fear and more like warning. A signal from somewhere deep and instinctive that whatever was happening on the other side of that wall was not like the other nights.

Something urged me out of my crib.

I tiptoed down to their room. The door wasn't fully closed. I remember the walk. I remember the nightlight plugged into the outlet in the hallway... the kind that casts a thin orange-yellow glow along the floor, almost like a small candle flame caught behind plastic. I moved the way children do when they understand, without being taught, that being seen or heard will change things. Careful. Quiet. Pressing myself to the edge of the doorframe so that whatever was happening inside that room would not know I was there.

Through the opening I could see just enough.

My mother was against the headboard of the waterbed, her body recoiled into the corner of it, her hands raised near her face. Not fighting. Just shielding. The posture of a person who has learned that shrinking is the only available protection. That the goal is no longer to stop what's coming but simply to survive it.

My father was standing over her.

His arm was extended. Rigid. Deliberate.

He had a gun pointed at her.

He was yelling. And with every sharp word, she flinched. Her whole body answered his voice like it was a physical thing... coiling, bracing, absorbing. He would yell and she would shrink. He would yell again and she would cover her face and wait for whatever came next. Over and over. The same brutal rhythm.

I stood there and I did not move.

I don't know for how long. I never announced myself. I never went in. Some part of me, even at that age, understood that walking through that door would only make things worse. So I stayed at the edge of the light. Watching. Scared in the way that stops the body from doing anything at all, where every instinct cancels every other instinct out and you end up frozen, just recording.

I knew what guns did. I'd seen enough television to understand, in the rough way that toddlers understand things, that the object in my father's hand was serious. That the situation in that room was operating at a level I didn't have a category for.

But I didn't need to fully understand the mechanics to understand the truth of what I was watching.

My mother was in danger. The person who was supposed to keep her safe was the one holding the weapon. And there was nothing a toddler standing in a hallway could do about any of it.

I don't remember leaving the doorway.

I just remember the image. Burned in the way a flashbulb leaves a ghost on the back of your eyes even after the light is gone. The extended arm. The rigid posture. Her hands covering her face. The flinch.

That image has never left.

It never will.

. . .

What I Actually Saw

Here is what I've come to understand about that moment, years and years removed from it:

I didn't only see a gun.

I saw anguish. I saw hopelessness in its most undisguised form. I saw what a person looks like when they have been worn down past the point of fighting back, past reasoning, past escape... when all that remains is the raw, animal work of getting through the next few minutes. No strategy. No plan. Just endurance.

I saw trust destroyed.

Not strained. Not damaged. Destroyed. The trust of a wife in her husband. The trust that is supposed to be the bedrock of a home, the thing that makes two people genuinely safe with each other. I watched it get shattered in real time, in the most complete and final way possible. And what was on her face in that moment was not anger, not defiance, not even fear in the conventional sense.

It was the face of a person who had stopped expecting anything better.

That is a different kind of devastation than fear. Fear at least holds the possibility of relief. What I saw was something that had moved past fear into a place where the hope of relief had been given up entirely. She wasn't waiting for it to stop because she believed it would stop. She was waiting because there was nothing else to do.

I didn't have language for any of that then. I was a toddler. But my body understood it. My eyes recorded it. Something in my nervous system filed it in a place that has never been fully accessible to me in the ordinary way that memories work... deeper than that, in the place where the things that fundamentally alter a person take up permanent residence.

What got deposited in me in that hallway was something I couldn't have named until I was much older.

Empathy.

Not the kind you learn from being taught to consider other people's feelings. Not the intellectual variety that you can study your way into.

The kind that gets pressed into you at the cellular level of recognition. The kind where pain sees pain and knows it immediately... not because you've read about it, not because you've been trained to identify it, but because you have been close enough to watch it happen to someone you loved when you were too small to do anything about it.

I can look into the eyes of someone who is carrying betrayal, anguish, the specific exhaustion of a person who has been surviving for too long... and I know it. Immediately. Not because I am perceptive in some general way. Because I have seen what those things look like in their most unfiltered, unperformed form. In the middle of the night. Through a cracked door. In a moment when no one was managing anything for anyone else's benefit.

No performance. No filter. Just the truth of what a human being looks like when they are completely broken.

I have seen it.

And that sight, as terrible as it was, became the foundation of something that has defined my ability to connect with people for the rest of my life. When someone sits across from me in pain, they don't have to explain it. They don't have to dress it up or make it legible or find the right words. Something in me already knows. Already recognizes. Already meets them there without having to travel very far.

That recognition was born in a hallway I never asked to walk down.

It is mine now.

And I have learned, slowly, to use it.

. . .

The Instinct to Bury It

For a long time, I did everything I could to make that night disappear.

Not consciously. Not with intention. The mind does what it has to do to keep you functional, and what mine did was build a wall around that memory as quickly as it could and then go about the business of survival. File it. Cover it. Stack enough ordinary days on top of it that the weight of regular life might eventually press it flat.

That is what I did.

For years.

I told myself I was past it. Told myself that I had processed it, or that there was nothing to process because it was a long time ago and I was fine and the evidence of my fine-ness was all around me. A business. A marriage. Kids who laughed at breakfast. A life that looked, from the outside, like someone who had figured things out.

I was not past it.

The image doesn't respond to time the way you want it to. It doesn't soften around the edges or lose its specificity with each passing year. It doesn't fade the way ordinary memories fade, dissolving into impressions and general feelings and the vague outlines of something that once happened. It stays sharp. Stays present. Stays exactly as specific as it was the night it was recorded.

It would surface without warning. Without invitation. Without any logical connection to whatever was happening around me. I would be working, or laughing with my kids, or driving in full daylight on a highway that had nothing to do with anything, and something would shift. A tone of voice. A particular quality of tension in a room. The way someone's body language changes when fear enters. And I would be right back there. Toddler-sized. Pressed against a doorframe. Watching something I could not stop and could not look away from.

And every time it surfaced, my response was the same.

Push it back down. File it deeper. Build the wall higher.

I became skilled at this. Genuinely skilled. I could feel the memory starting to surface and I could redirect my attention before it fully arrived. I could stay three steps ahead of it, keeping busy enough and loud enough and productive enough that there was never enough silence for it to fully land.

What I didn't understand then, and what I had to learn the hard way, is this:

There is a difference between burying something and carrying it underground.

Buried things decompose. They break down. They return to the earth and become something else over time. That is what we mean when we say we want to bury the past.

But what we actually do... what I actually did... is carry it underground. Unchanged. Intact. Exactly as heavy as it was the day we decided we didn't want to feel it anymore. We just made it invisible. We took the weight and moved it somewhere no one else could see it.

The invisible weight is the most exhausting kind.

Because you cannot put down what no one else can see. You can't be helped with it. You can't share it. You can't set it on a table and look at it with another person and decide together what to do with it. You just carry it alone, in the dark, for as long as you are willing to keep pretending it isn't there.

I carried it alone for a long time.

Too long.

And here is the other thing about carrying it underground that took me even longer to understand:

It doesn't just cost you. It costs the people around you.

The weight shows up in other rooms. It shows up in the way you react to certain tones of voice. In the hypervigilance you bring to spaces where there is no actual threat. In the emotional distance you create when things start to feel too familiar, too close to something you filed away years ago and still haven't looked at directly. The people you love feel the weight even when they can't see it. They live with the effects of it without ever being handed an explanation.

You tell yourself you're protecting them.

You are also, quietly, keeping yourself alone with something that was never meant to be carried alone.

. . .

The Conversation in the Dark

My mother never knew I was there that night.

For years, that memory belonged only to me. She carried her version of it... whatever she carried from that room, from that night, from everything that came before and after. I carried mine. And the two of us built a life alongside each other with that shared history sitting between us, unspoken, unacknowledged, occupying space in both of our lives without either of us ever naming it.

Then one evening, as a teenager, I brought it up.

I don't fully remember how I introduced it. What I remember is where we were. The living room. After dark. The television throwing its low blue-gray light across the room, catching the cigarette smoke that drifted in thin, lazy curls through the air between us. That particular kind of half-lit quiet that a house has at the end of a long day, when the edges of things go soft and the walls feel closer than they do in daylight.

I said something. Some version of: I remember that night. The hallway. The gun.

And I honestly wish I had never said anything.

Not because it wasn't real. It was real. Memories like that don't appear from nothing. You don't construct a gun at your mother's temple out of the imagination of a toddler. Some things don't fade because they are not supposed to. I was certain of what I saw then and I am certain of it now.

But I wish I hadn't said anything because of what happened to her face when I did.

She tried to deny it at first. The words came out soft and uncertain, the way a person speaks when they are hoping that saying the opposite of a thing will make the thing less true. "No... no, that didn't happen." Not a lie. A prayer. But even as the words left her, I could see the memory moving back into her. Years of trying to keep that night at a distance, years of building an entire life on the other side of it, and here it was, called up again by her teenage son sitting a few feet away in the dark.

The denial didn't hold. The memory was already back.

And then I saw it.

The terror.

The same terror that had been in her eyes that night in that room, with the gun at her temple... it came back. Right there in the living room. In the television light and the cigarette smoke. It moved across her face like a current, like something electric and involuntary, something her body remembered before her mind had fully caught up.

But it was not the same terror. That night, she had been afraid for her own life. Standing in her own hallway, her husband's arm extended, the cold logic of that gun making everything else irrelevant.

This terror was different.

This one was for me.

In the space of a few seconds, the thing she was afraid of had shifted entirely. She wasn't afraid of him anymore. She was afraid of what had been done to her son. Afraid that the cost of that night hadn't been paid by her... that it had been paid by a toddler standing in a dark hallway who she hadn't known was there. That her child had been carrying something this heavy, this specific, this sharp... and she had not known. All those years, and she had not known.

I watched that land on her.

A mother's grief has a particular quality. It doesn't look like ordinary sadness. It looks like someone absorbing a weight that they would give anything to carry themselves, if it meant the person they love didn't have to. It looks like someone doing the math on years of not knowing and arriving at a number too large to hold.

She looked at me in that low light and that smoky air, and all she wanted to do was go back. To that hallway. To that night. To stand between me and the doorframe and make sure I never saw what I saw.

She couldn't.

Nobody could.

We sat with that for a while. The television kept going. The smoke kept drifting. Neither of us said much more. There wasn't much to say. Some things don't have a resolution. They just have a moment when two people finally acknowledge them, in the same room, at the same time, and that acknowledgment has to be enough.

It was enough.

I wish I had never brought it up, because of what it cost her to remember.

I am also glad I did, because of what it meant to finally not carry it alone.

She loved me with everything she had in circumstances that had already exceeded everything she had.

She was enough.

She always was.

. . .

The Bright Side

Here is the thing about pain that no one tells you when you are in the middle of it:

It is not random.

I spent years believing that what happened in that hallway was a wound and nothing more. Evidence of a childhood that was unfair, a thing that happened to me that I did not deserve and could not change and simply had to find a way to live around. Those things are true. I am not going to minimize them or dress them in borrowed meaning or rush past the grief to get to the lesson.

The grief is real. The damage is real. The cost was real.

And alongside all of that... this is also true:

God did not waste what happened to me.

That is the sentence I had to sit with for a long time. The question I asked for years with anger, with tears, in the particular silence that arrives when you have asked something so many times that you have stopped expecting an answer:

Why did You let that happen?

Why that night? Why that hallway? Why did You allow a toddler to see that... to carry that... to grow up with that image burned into the back of his eyes like a brand he didn't ask for and couldn't remove?

I asked that question with anger. I asked it with grief. I asked it in the middle of success, when by every external measure I had no right to still be haunted, and the haunting came anyway, and the question came with it.

The answer didn't come as an argument. It didn't come as a theological explanation that made the pain feel proportionate to the purpose. It didn't come loudly or dramatically or with any of the fanfare you might hope for when you've been waiting on an answer for decades.

It came quietly. The way the most important things usually do.

Your pain may not be for you.

Read that again. Slowly.

Your pain may not be for you.

It may be for the person who is standing right now in their own hallway. Who is watching something they cannot un-see. Who will spend the next decade trying to bury it, carrying it underground, pretending it isn't still sharp and present and surfacing at 2 a.m. without warning. Who has never heard another person say out loud the thing they have only dared to think alone in the dark.

That person needs a witness.

Not a therapist, though therapy has its place. Not a book with clinical language, though those have their place too. Not someone who studied what they went through from a safe and professional distance.

Someone who was actually there.

Someone who was small enough to still be in a crib. Who walked down a hallway toward a light they didn't fully understand. Who pressed themselves against a doorframe and watched something that no child should ever have to watch and then spent years trying to make it disappear.

Someone who came out the other side anyway.

Someone who can look them in the eyes and say, without flinching: I know. I've been there. Not approximately. Not metaphorically. There.

That is not something that can be manufactured. It cannot be studied into existence or earned through good intentions or approximated by someone who cares deeply but has never actually stood in that hallway.

It has to be real. And it is real. Because you were there.

The story you have been trying to hide... the memory that keeps surfacing no matter how deep you file it... the chapter of your life that you have edited and minimized and buried because the true version feels like too much to ask of anyone... that story might be the exact lifeline that someone, somewhere, is desperately praying for.

Not a version of it. Not a cleaned-up, softened, made-presentable summary of it.

The real one. With the specific details. The nightlight in the hallway. The waterbed. The extended arm. The flinch.

The truth has to be specific enough to recognize. If it isn't specific, it can't reach the specific person who needs it. They will read something general and think: that's not quite what happened to me. They will feel the almost of it and remain alone with their exact thing.

But when the truth is specific... when someone reads something and thinks, that's my hallway, that's my nightlight, that's my version of that night... the isolation breaks. Not slowly. Immediately. The wall that has been keeping them alone with it develops a crack, and through that crack comes the first real air they've breathed on the subject in years.

You are that crack in the wall for someone.

Your specific, undisguised, hard-to-write, harder-to-say story is the thing that lets another person stop being alone with theirs.

That is not a small thing.

That is not an accident.

Pain that is kept in the dark stays a wound.

Pain that is carried into the light becomes a bridge.

The thing you most want to forget may be the most important thing about you. Not the most comfortable. Not the thing you would choose to lead with. But the most important in this specific and irreplaceable way: it qualifies you to reach the person no one else can reach. It gives you access to rooms that are closed to everyone who hasn't been there.

Walk through those rooms.

Say the true thing.

Let the specificity of your pain become the precision instrument that finds exactly the person who needed to hear it.

That is the bright side of what cannot be un-seen.

Not that it didn't hurt.

Not that the cost was small.

But that it was not wasted. And that you are not done with it yet.

The best use of your story is still ahead of you.

. . .

CHOOSE YOURSELF ... YOU'RE WORTH THE RESCUE

You've read what I saw. What I heard. What got deposited in me before I was old enough to have a word for any of it.

The screams through trailer walls. The metallic smell of blood. A gun pressed to my mother's temple. These are the images that opened this story, and I don't share them to shock you. I share them because they are the ground this chapter grows out of. Because what happened next ... what my mother finally chose ... didn't come out of nowhere. It came out of all of that.

Every breaking point has a history.

And sometimes the history has to get heavy enough before the body finally says: no more.

. . .

The One Line He Never Crossed

There is something I've never fully said out loud, and I want to say it here.

My father never hit me.

In a chapter full of violence, that detail matters. I've thought about it more times than I can count, trying to understand it. A man who could do what he did to my mother ... consistently, deliberately, without remorse ... somehow never turned that toward me. I don't think it was restraint in any noble sense. I don't think it was love, exactly. I think it was something closer to self-preservation.

Because my mother told me ... more than once, and in considerable detail ... what she would have done if he had.

She said it calmly. That was the part that stayed with me. Not rage. Not desperation. Calm. The kind of calm that comes from a decision already made, a line already drawn so deeply it doesn't need to be defended out loud ... only stated.

She would have killed him.

And I believed her. I still do. I think some part of him believed it too. Which means that somewhere underneath the cruelty, underneath the drinking and the fists and the years of systematic destruction ... he understood consequence. He understood that there was exactly one thing that would cost him everything.

Hurting me.

Sometimes I wonder if she was planning it. Not as a fantasy. As a contingency. As the locked-and-loaded answer to a question she prayed he would never force her to ask.

I can't blame her. I won't blame her. She was living inside something most people will never fully understand, and she was building whatever armor she could out of whatever materials were available.

. . .

The Pattern That Became the Weather

My mother told me, before she passed, that she had tried to leave several times. That the night I'm about to describe was not the first time she had packed herself up in her mind and pointed toward the door. She had gotten to the threshold more than once. Had stood at the edge of it, looking out at whatever unknown existed on the other side, and then ... gone back.

Because he would beg.

That's the part nobody talks about. The part that makes people on the outside say things like: why didn't she just leave? As if leaving were a simple calculation. As if the man who hit her wasn't also the man who, in the aftermath, became someone else entirely. Someone who kneeled. Who wept. Who promised, with everything he had, that it would be different this time.

She believed in the warmth she'd seen in him once. She kept believing it was still in there somewhere, buried under the damage, waiting to come back. And every time she went back, every time she gave that belief another chance ... the warmth would hold for a while.

And then the chill would return.

The wrath would fall, and the whole cycle would begin again. And the next time he begged, there was less warmth to believe in and more evidence to weigh against it.

This is how it went. For years. This is how it goes for a lot of people. Not because they are weak. Not because they don't know better. But because love is complicated and hope is stubborn and leaving takes more than a decision ... it takes a moment. The right one. A window that opens.

. . .

A Typical Night

He would come home from work.

Something would happen. It didn't take much. A word. A look. The particular way dinner was sitting on the table, or wasn't. Some internal weather system that had been building all day, needing only the smallest excuse to release.

He would leave for the bar.

That was the exhale before the storm. The house would get quiet in his absence, but it wasn't peaceful quiet. It was the quiet of people waiting. Of two people making themselves smaller, softer, less available as targets ... as if that had ever helped. The television would murmur at a volume chosen not for enjoyment, but for cover. My mother's eyes would drift toward the window. Toward the driveway. Measuring the absence, knowing it was temporary.

He would come back.

The truck in the driveway was a sound you felt before you heard it. The particular rumble of that engine had a weight to it. And in the seconds between hearing it and the door opening, something would happen to the air inside that trailer. It would change. The way the air changes before lightning ... that charged, breathless stillness.

And then he would do what he did.

And then ... usually ... he would take me.

That was the ritual. After the violence, after my mother lay broken somewhere in that trailer, he would scoop me up and we'd go. A convenience store. A toy. Necco wafers with their chalky pastel sweetness that tasted wrong even when I didn't have the words to say why. I've written about that elsewhere in this book. The counterfeit kindness. The way he used me to clean his hands of what he'd just done. Sugar and plastic trucks as receipts for guilt.

That ritual served him. I understand that now. It got him out of the house. It put distance between himself and what he'd done. And it kept me ... for a little while, in a store lit up with fluorescent light ... from seeing my mother on the floor.

But this night was different.

This night, after the abuse, he didn't take me anywhere.

He just ... passed out.

That's it. That's the whole difference. The tiny deviation in a terrible pattern that changed everything. No trip to the store. No candy. No ritual to close the loop and buy himself a few hours of something that felt like normal. Just the violence, and then silence, and then the slack breathing of a man who had exhausted himself on cruelty and had nothing left.

My mother looked at that silence.

And she recognized it for what it was.

A window.

. . .

The Night the Window Opened

I don't know the exact trigger that particular night. What I know is that the pattern ran its course, and when it was done, when the house went still and his breathing slowed into the slack rhythm of someone who was out ... my mother looked at me.

And she made a decision.

Not a long one. Not a carefully reasoned, fully planned decision. Those don't exist inside situations like this. What she made was an instant one. The kind that arrives from somewhere below the thinking mind ... from the part of a person that has been adding up evidence for years and has finally reached a sum it cannot ignore.

Enough.

She didn't pack. There was no time for packing, no room for the noise of it. She grabbed a coat. She took my hand.

That was it. That was all she took.

Years of a life in that trailer ... whatever small accumulations of furniture, photographs, clothing, the ordinary objects that make up a home ... she left all of it. Left the coffee mugs on the shelf. Left the photos on the wall. Left whatever remained of the life she'd believed in when she first moved into that place. Because the alternative was to stay one more night inside something that was killing her. And she had finally reached the place where leaving ... even with nothing, even into cold and uncertainty ... was the only choice she could live with.

I didn't know it as we walked out the door, but I was leaving that trailer for the last time. I would never set foot in it again.

. . .

Underneath the Landing

Northeast Ohio winter doesn't negotiate. It commits. The kind of cold that finds every gap in your coat, every unguarded inch of skin, and reminds you it was here long before you were and will be here long after. The kind of cold that doesn't just chill you ... it settles in. Makes itself at home inside your chest.

We were crouched beneath the landing outside the front door. Not hiding in any dramatic sense. Hiding the way hunted things hide. Pressed flat against whatever cover existed, barely breathing, trying to take up as little space as possible in the frozen dark.

The ground beneath us was hard. The kind of cold Ohio dirt that has surrendered every drop of warmth it was carrying and has nothing left to give. I remember the feel of it through whatever I had on. The particular stillness of air so cold it makes your eyes water without wind.

My mother's body was trembling.

Not from the cold.

She was holding me so tightly I could feel her heartbeat. Fast. Uneven. A rhythm that said: we are not safe yet. Her arms around me were not soft comfort. They were grip. The grip of a person who is holding the only thing she is certain about in that moment, which was me.

She whispered in my ear.

"Shhhhh ... "

That sound. That specific, barely-there exhale of a mother trying to keep her child quiet because she can hear him moving around inside. I didn't fully understand what we were doing. I understood her body. I understood her voice. And both of them said: be still, be quiet, don't make a sound.

We don't know what woke him. Maybe the demons that lived in his head, always restless, never fully quiet. Maybe the hiss of the screen door and the soft thump of it closing behind us. However it happened ... he was awake. And he was moving. And then we could hear him calling for her, his voice starting somewhere between groggy and angry and climbing fast toward something worse.

My mother picked me up. Pressed herself back against the foundation of the trailer, making herself as small as she possibly could. Her arms were shaking. Her breath came in shallow pulls, controlled, almost silent.

The door burst open above us.

He stood on the landing. His feet ... inches from our heads.

I remember looking up. The streetlight from the road cast his silhouette down onto the ground beside us ... a long, angular shape stretched across the frozen dirt. I stared at it the way a child stares at something they can't fully categorize. My small mind trying to hold two things at once that didn't belong together.

Fear, yes. My mother was trembling against me and my body understood threat even when my mind couldn't name it.

But also ... he was my dad.

Even then. Even crouched in the dark with her body coiled against mine. Some young and honest part of me loved him. Didn't understand him. Couldn't have articulated any of it. But loved him the way children love the people who are supposed to love them back, without any guarantee the feeling goes both ways. That grief was already forming. I just didn't have a word for it yet.

He yelled into the empty night. The sound of it bouncing off the trailers nearby, swallowed by the cold. Then he stumbled down the steps. Got into his van. And drove away.

The taillights ... red against the dark, bleeding smaller and smaller down the road until they disappeared.

My mother didn't move for a long time after that. She was listening. Making sure the sound didn't return. When she finally exhaled, the breath came out shaky and long ... like something she'd been holding since before that night. Maybe since before I was born.

I don't know exactly how we got to my grandparents' house. The details of that drive are not something my memory kept. What I know is that we made it. And when we did, I got to just be a kid. Safe. Unhidden. Not measuring the temperature of every room before walking into it.

My mother began, slowly, the long work of starting over.

This would be the last time I saw my father for several years.

. . .

The Confusing Truth

I was glad.

I was also sad.

Both of those things were true at the same time, and nobody prepared me for that. Nobody told me relief and grief could share the same moment without canceling each other out. That you could be grateful to be free and still feel the absence of the person you escaped from.

He was my dad. And even though what he brought with him was destruction ... even though the house was quieter and safer without him ... the hole was still real. A child-shaped grief that had no clean name.

I didn't have a word for it then. I've found words for it since.

Both things can be true. They don't cancel each other. They just coexist, like two rooms inside the same house, and you learn to live with both doors open at once.

. . .

What She Was Really Choosing

Leaving was not just a physical act. It was a declaration.

In the time this happened, leaving your husband was not a celebrated decision. It wasn't met with a support system or a chorus of encouragement. It was met with questions. With judgment. With the particular cruelty that communities reserve for women who don't stay. What will people say. What kind of woman leaves. You made your bed.

She left anyway.

With nothing but a coat and my hand and whatever she could carry inside her.

There is a belief that lives inside a lot of people who grow up in chaos. It isn't loud. It doesn't announce itself. It just sits underneath everything else and quietly shapes every decision from the basement of the self.

The belief is this: I'm not worth the rescue.

It shows up in different disguises. Sometimes it sounds like: others have it worse. Sometimes it sounds like: I brought this on myself. Sometimes it sounds like: this is just how things are. Sometimes it sounds like nothing at all … it just shows up as a slowness to act, a reluctance to reach, a settled-in resignation to less than you deserve.

My mother answered that belief with her body on a frozen Ohio night. She answered it without knowing she was answering it. Without a speech or a declaration or a plan she'd spent weeks rehearsing.

She just moved.

And that movement said: we matter. Our lives have value that outweighs the risk of this step. Whatever is on the other side of that van pulling away is worth more than one more night of this.

She was right.

. . .

The Bright Side

I want to tell you she was free after that. That the moment we pulled away from that trailer, the weight lifted and the healing began and the story turned toward light.

Some of it did.

But some scars don't heal on a timeline. Some wounds don't close just because the source of them is gone. Abuse doesn't stop when the door shuts behind you. It lingers. It follows. It shows up in the way you flinch at certain sounds, in the way you brace for impact in rooms where there is no danger, in the patterns you carry forward into the next chapter of your life without fully realizing you brought them along.

My mother had escaped the man. She had not yet escaped what he'd done to her. That work ... the work of becoming someone who isn't still living inside that trailer even when you're somewhere else entirely ... that work was still ahead. And it would be harder than leaving. Slower. Less visible.

But here is what I know.

Choosing yourself is not selfish.

Read that again if you need to.

It is not selfish.

It is the prerequisite.

You cannot heal from inside the thing that is hurting you. You cannot grow inside a space that has no room for growth. You cannot become who you are meant to become while every ounce of your energy is being poured into surviving what you should not have to survive in the first place.

Choosing yourself is the first act of healing. Not the last one. Not the reward you receive after you've done enough work to deserve it. The first one. The act that makes every other act possible.

My mother didn't know she was doing something profound that night. She was just trying to survive. She was doing what survival required. But in choosing to move ... in refusing to let one more night become her whole story ... she gave me something I have been passing forward ever since.

Permission.

Permission to say: this isn't working and I deserve better. Permission to walk toward something unknown because the known thing has already cost too much. Permission to believe that starting over on shaky ground is still starting over, and that shaky ground is still ground.

You are allowed to choose yourself.

Not as an act of abandonment. Not as a way of turning your back on people you love. But as an act of fidelity ... to the self you were meant to become, to the life you were built to live, to the story that doesn't have to end in that driveway on a winter night.

The healing does not begin when the conditions are perfect. It doesn't begin when you have a plan, when the finances are stable, when the right words finally come, when the guilt finally lifts. The healing begins the moment you decide that you are worth the effort of it. That your life ... this one, the only one you have ... is worth protecting.

That moment can be right now.

You don't need the circumstances to cooperate. You need the conviction. Even a thin one. Even one that's trembling. Even one that's sitting beneath a landing in the dark, heartbeat going too fast, waiting for taillights to disappear.

Conviction doesn't have to be loud to be real.

My mother's was barely a whisper. It was nothing more than a coat grabbed off a hook and a small hand held in the dark.

And it was enough.

It was more than enough.

Starting over on shaky ground is still starting over. A fresh start built on the ruins of something broken is still a fresh start. The scar tissue you carry from what you survived is not evidence that you are too damaged for something better. It is evidence that you are strong enough to have survived it at all.

You are worth the rescue.

Not after you prove it. Not once you've earned it back. Not when you've suffered long enough to justify the attempt.

Now. As you are. With everything you're carrying and everything you're afraid of and everything you still can't explain.

You were worth it the moment you were born. That has never changed.

She knew it then. She knew it until the day she passed.

I know it too.

And if you are standing at any version of that door right now ... if you are crouching beneath any version of that landing, holding your breath, wondering if the other side is worth the risk ...

It is.

Walk toward the light you can see. Let the rest come.

. . .

CHAPTER FIVE

BORROWED BELIEF
IS STILL BELIEF

Chapter Four ended with taillights.

With a frozen Ohio night and two people pressed beneath a landing, hearts going too fast, waiting for danger to disappear down the road.

With a mother who grabbed a coat and her child's hand and chose the unknown over one more night of the known.

That was the first act of freedom.

But freedom, it turns out, is not a destination. It is a direction. And the distance between leaving something and actually being free of it... that distance is longer than any of us want it to be. The road out of a storm does not end the moment the storm stops. The body keeps the weather. The nervous system keeps the record. The child who learned to read danger in the creak of a door does not unlearn that overnight simply because the door is different now.

What we left behind that night was the source of the violence.

What we carried with us... that was something else entirely.

. . .

Finding the Floor Again

My grandparents' house was the first place I remember feeling safe.

Not because anything dramatic happened there. Not because it was big or extraordinary or because someone sat me down and told me everything was going to be okay. It was safe the way a harbor is safe. Not because of anything it does, but because of what it is. Steady. Quiet. A place where the air doesn't change when a car pulls into the driveway.

I remember the particular quality of that stillness. The way a house feels when the people in it are not bracing for impact. I had spent most of my young life in spaces where tension was the weather... where every room had an invisible pressure in it, where I had learned to measure the atmosphere before I walked through any door. I didn't even know I was doing it. That's how early the habit forms. It becomes invisible to you, because it has never not been there.

At my grandparents', I started to forget to do it.

That sounds small. It was not small. It was enormous. The beginning of something I didn't have a name for yet... the slow and fragile process of learning how to exist in a space without waiting for it to turn on you.

My mother was doing her own version of the same thing.

I would watch her during those first weeks and months. The way she moved through a day. There was a tentative quality to it, like someone who has been underwater for a long time and has just broken the surface and is not yet sure the air is going to keep being there. She was working.

She was building. She was doing all the things survival requires… finding a job, creating a structure, carving out some small version of a life that was hers instead of something she was enduring.

But I could see the other thing, too.

At night, mostly. When the busyness of the day ran out and the quiet arrived, and there was nothing left to do but be. I would catch glimpses of it in the way she sat. In the distance that would come into her eyes. In the moments when she was in the room but also somewhere else entirely, somewhere I couldn't follow, working through something that had no easy resolution.

When you leave someone you once loved… when you leave someone who was also, somewhere underneath the damage, the person you had chosen… the leaving does not answer all the questions. It answers the immediate one: am I safe tonight? But it opens up others. Ones that don't have clean answers. Ones that arrive in the dark when the house is quiet and the kids are asleep and there is nothing left to distract you from the weight of everything that happened and everything that didn't.

She carried those questions.

I could see them in her, even if I didn't understand them. Even a child reads the emotional truth of the people they love. Long before you have language for it, you have perception. And what I perceived in my mother during those early months was a woman who was brave and exhausted and grieving things that didn't have names yet.

The light was coming back. Slowly. Unevenly. The way light always comes back after the kind of dark she had been inside.

But it was coming.

. . .

Learning What Quiet Could Mean

I started preschool around that time.

The preschool was right behind the apartment we eventually moved into, close enough that I could walk. This was the world in those days... children moved through neighborhoods on their own two feet, were trusted with the small geography of their immediate surroundings. I walked to preschool. I walked home. The routine of it was its own kind of education.

I remember liking it. The particular small-scale world of a preschool, with its low tables and bright colors and the specific warm smell of crayons and construction paper. It was the first environment I could remember that was designed entirely around being a child... where the furniture was the right size, where the expectations were manageable, where nobody in the room was operating at a register that set off alarms in the body.

I was learning, without knowing I was learning, what it felt like to just... exist. To take up space without managing it. To be four years old and have that be enough.

I had a toy.

This detail matters more than it might seem, so I want to give it the space it deserves.

It was a transformer. A submarine, specifically. The kind of toy that was nothing and everything at the same time... plastic, simple, probably bought for a few dollars somewhere. But this one I carried everywhere.

It lived in my pocket. I would take it out and turn it over in my hands and the feel of it was grounding in the way that only a child's beloved object can be grounding. It was mine. In a life that had given me very little that was certain, this thing was certain. It was there when I reached for it.

Which is why what happened on one of those walks home hit as hard as it did.

A girl from the apartment building stopped me.

She was bigger. Or at least she seemed bigger, the way anyone seems bigger when you are small and they are between you and where you want to go. There was a confrontation, the kind that happens in the particular social ecosystem of small children who have not yet learned all the rules of how to exist alongside each other. She roughed me up. And then she took my transformer... my submarine, my pocketed certainty, the thing I reached for when I needed something solid... and she threw it down.

It shattered.

I remember the sound. The scatter of plastic pieces across the pavement. The irreversibility of it.

I came home devastated in the way that only a four-year-old can be devastated, which is to say completely, without the benefit of perspective or the cognitive tools to locate the feeling in any larger context. It was not just a broken toy. It was the thing I loved, gone. And coming from a childhood that had already asked me to give up a great deal... coming from a life where things of value had a way of not lasting... it landed harder than it might have landed on another child in different circumstances.

I was four years old and I was heartbroken.

. . .

The Question That Changed Everything

My mother's boyfriend sat me down.

He had come into our lives gradually, the way the right things tend to arrive... not with announcement, not with drama, but quietly, steadily, showing up in the small ways that over time accumulate into something significant. He was an old school friend of my mother's. Someone she had known before the years of the storm. Someone from a chapter of her life that predated everything that had gone wrong.

His name was Rob.

I want to be clear about what he was at this point in the story, because it matters for how you read everything that follows. He was not yet my stepfather. That title came later, after time had been spent and trust had been earned and something real had been built between all of us. At this point he was simply the man my mother had reconnected with. Her boyfriend. A presence that was becoming steadier and more constant in ways I was still learning to measure.

But I'll tell you this: he would become my stepfather. And the reason he could was largely because of the way he handled the very early days... the way he moved slowly, without assumption, without pushing his way into a role he hadn't yet earned. He let the relationship find its own pace. He showed up without demanding to be seen. And over time, what started as a man my mother smiled at became something none of us could have planned but all of us needed.

That is getting ahead of ourselves a little. But I want the reader to know where this is going, because the moment I'm about to describe... the moment he sat me down and asked me a question... lands differently when you understand that this was a man in the process of becoming something more. Not just my mother's choice. Mine too, eventually.

I had watched him the way a child watches a new adult in their world... carefully, from a slight distance, reading every gesture for information. I had learned early how to do that. It had been a survival skill. You watch how a person enters a room. You watch what their hands do when they are frustrated. You watch whether their good moods and their bad moods come with the same eyes, or whether one of them is carrying something darker underneath.

His eyes were the same. That was the first thing I registered, even without the words to articulate it. Whatever mood he walked in with, the eyes were not hiding something else behind it. There was no second frequency running underneath the surface, no charge in the air when he moved through a space. Just a person. Present. Taking up no more room than was his.

He sat across from me while I was still shaking from what had happened on that walk home.

And he asked me a question I was not prepared for.

He asked: do you want this to happen again?

I remember looking at him. Because it was not the question I expected. I expected comfort. I expected sympathy. I expected someone to tell me it was going to be okay, to patch the thing with reassurance the way adults often do when a child is hurting and the hurt is something they don't know how to fix.

Instead he handed me a question.

And the question was about power.

Not power in the aggressive sense. Not power as something you take or impose. Power in the most basic and elemental sense: the recognition that you have control. That you are not only a thing that events happen to. That there is, inside you, a choice. A say in what direction your life goes, even when you are small, even when everything around you feels larger than you are.

Do you want this to happen again?

No. Obviously no. Of course I didn't.

He smiled. And then he said: let me show you something.

. . .

The Dragon

He had a VHS tape.

This was the era before DVDs, before streaming, before the entire library of human cinema was available on a device in your pocket. A VHS tape was a physical object... a black plastic brick that you inserted into a machine and waited for to rewind. He put it in.

And for the first time in my life, I watched Enter the Dragon.

I want to be careful about how I describe this moment, because it would be easy to inflate it into something cinematic. The truth is simpler than that, and simpler is more honest. I was four years old. I did not fully understand what I was watching. I didn't have the context or the vocabulary for it.

But something happened anyway.

What I saw on that screen was not what I expected. I was used to the idea that power looked a certain way. That it was large. That it was loud. That it announced itself by taking up room and making noise and making people afraid. That was the version of power I had grown up observing. That was the only model I had.

Bruce Lee was not large. He was not loud.

He was quiet in a way I had never associated with strength before. Controlled. Precise. Moving through the world with an economy of motion that communicated something I couldn't name at four but felt immediately: this is a person who is entirely in command of himself. Not of other people. Of himself. And that command... that interior steadiness... was the source of everything.

The people around him were louder. Bigger, in some cases. Angrier. More desperate.

He was still.

And the stillness was more powerful than any of the noise.

I had never seen that before. I had grown up believing, without knowing I believed it, that the loudest person in the room was the most powerful one. That fists and volume and the ability to make others afraid were what strength actually was. My entire frame of reference for what a powerful man looked like had been built around a man who used those tools.

This was different.

This was the first time I understood, at whatever level a four-year-old can understand anything, that strength and violence are not the same thing. That a person could be formidable and still. That power does not have to take anything from anyone. That the most dangerous thing in a room might be the quietest.

Rob asked if I wanted to learn.

I nodded so fast I nearly fell off the couch.

. . .

The Dojo

The gym was not what I expected, though I'm not sure what I expected.

It was small. Functional in the way that places built around purpose tend to be functional, without excess or decoration. The floors were worn in the specific way that floors get worn when people have trained on them for years... a kind of lived-in smoothness that told you something serious had been happening here for a long time. The smell was sweat and ambition and the particular dusty warmth of a space that had been breathed in and breathed out by hundreds of people working toward something.

There were not many kids.

This was not a children's program. This was an adult gym that accepted children as participants in the same classes. Which meant you were expected to keep up. You were expected to listen, to try, to execute. Nobody was going to slow the pace because you were small. The standard existed and you rose to meet it, or you didn't, and the rising was the point.

I remember feeling scared.

Not the same kind of scared I had felt in that trailer. That fear had been shapeless and large, a whole-body response to a threat that existed everywhere and came without warning. This was a different quality of fear entirely. Smaller. More specific. The fear of a child who has entered a room where something difficult is being asked and is not yet sure they are capable of it.

That kind of fear, I would learn, is useful. It means you are exactly at the edge of what you know. It means growth is close.

I bowed in for the first time.

There is something in that gesture that I didn't understand then but have spent years thinking about since. The bow is not submission. It is acknowledgment. It says: I am entering a space where something is being offered, and I am coming in with respect for what that offering costs. It is the gesture of someone who understands that learning requires a particular posture. That you cannot fill a vessel that is already insisting it is full.

I bowed in, and I began.

The Sensei was a high school friend of Rob's... a man who had been training since before I was born and had poured that training into a gym and a system and a way of teaching that had shaped more people than he probably knew. He was not soft. He was not gentle in the way that gentleness is sometimes confused for kindness. He was demanding. He held a standard and he expected you to work toward it.

But here is what I had never encountered before, and what stopped me cold the first time I witnessed it:

He used his voice to build things.

I had grown up in a house where adult voices were instruments of destruction. Where volume was a weapon and tone was a threat and the emotional register of the room was something you monitored the way you monitor weather. I had never, in my early memory, been in a space where an adult raised their voice and the purpose of it was to lift someone up.

I watched him do it.

A student struggling with a technique. The Sensei's voice going louder... not in anger, not in frustration, but in encouragement. Pushing toward something. Saying, in effect, with volume and conviction: you are capable of more than you are currently attempting. I believe that. I am going to make you believe it too.

And the student tried harder.

And then did it.

I remember the feeling that moved through me watching that exchange. I didn't have a word for it. I was four. But it was something like: oh. So this is what a voice can do. Not tear down. Not threaten. Not make a person smaller. A voice can do this other thing. It can tell someone the truth about themselves when they've forgotten it. It can be the thing that gets someone to the other side of their own doubt.

I knew in that moment, without knowing I knew it, what I wanted to become.

Not a fighter. Not someone skilled solely in the mechanics of combat, though that would come.

A person who used their voice to build.

I just didn't know yet how long the road to that was, or how much of the journey still lay ahead.

. . .

What Rob Was Doing

My mother's boyfriend was not a dramatic person.

He didn't announce himself. He didn't come in with a speech or a set of intentions or a deliberately chosen program for how he was going to handle being a male presence in a small boy's life. He just showed up. Consistently. In the way that people show up when they are actually present rather than performing presence.

I have thought about him a great deal over the years. About what he did and how he did it, and about what it meant at the time versus what I understand it to mean now.

What he did, in the plainest terms, was this: he handed me a choice.

That question... do you want this to happen again... sounds simple. It is not simple. Embedded in that question is an entire philosophy. It is the assumption that you have a say. That what happens to you is not entirely beyond your influence. That the story of your life is not something being written entirely by forces outside you, but something you are participating in, even when you are very small, even when the situation feels completely outside your control.

For a child who had spent his early years in an environment where things happened to people... where the adults around him were largely subject to forces they couldn't manage, where the mood of one man could determine the safety of an entire household... that assumption was revolutionary.

He handed me control in a situation where I had felt none.

He didn't lecture. He didn't explain. He asked a question, waited for the honest answer, and then pointed toward a path. A VHS tape on a Tuesday evening. A drive to a gym. A man who used his voice to build.

That's all it was.

And it was more than enough.

There is a particular kind of person in this world... and if you have been fortunate enough to encounter one, you know exactly what I mean... who seems to understand instinctively that what a broken person needs is not to have their brokenness managed, but to be shown they are capable of more than they currently believe. These people don't try to fix you. They don't treat your damage as the primary fact about you, the thing that has to be addressed and resolved before anything else can happen. They simply see more of you than you can currently see of yourself. And they hold that larger vision steady while you work your way toward it.

Rob was that for me.

My mother had chosen well. I didn't have the capacity to understand that at four. I do now.

. . .

What I Brought Through the Door

Here is the honest part.

I walked into that gym carrying everything. Every night in that trailer. Every sound through thin walls. Every Necco Wafer that tasted wrong. The gun barrel I had seen at three years old, burned into the back of my eyes where it has lived ever since. The particular shape of terror that was my mother's body against a headboard. The milk crate in the van. The way I had been conditioned to associate his damage with something that sometimes felt like love.

I didn't walk in clean. Nobody does.

We never arrive anywhere clean. We arrive carrying the full weight of everything that made us, which means the full weight of the hardest things we survived, and we try to find in the new place something that the old place never gave us. We are always, in some way, bringing the storm into the harbor with us.

What the martial arts did... and I want to be careful here, because this is not a simple story and I don't want to make it one... is not erase any of that. It did not undo what had been done. It did not close the wounds or answer the questions or resolve the grief that was still working its way through me in ways I couldn't have articulated.

What it did was give me a container.

A place where the energy generated by all of those years had somewhere to go. A structure that held me. A practice that asked me to show up fully and work hard and be present in my body in a way that was new and demanding and... good. Something that was good. Something that was mine.

And it gave me a mirror.

When the Sensei's voice said: you are capable of more than you are currently attempting... and I pushed past what I thought my limit was and discovered there was more on the other side of it... something shifted in the story I was telling myself about who I was. Not dramatically. Not all at once. But incrementally, over weeks and months, a different narrative began to form.

Not: I am the child of what happened in that trailer.

But: I am someone who can learn. Someone who can improve. Someone who can, through effort and discipline and showing up, become more than I currently am.

Those two narratives exist inside the same person. They still do. But one of them had been so dominant for so long that the other one had barely had room to breathe.

The dojo gave it room.

. . .

The New Shape of a Day

I want to describe what life looked like during this period, because the texture of it matters.

My mother was working. Building something new. The apartment was small and simple and nothing about it was remarkable except that it was ours and it was safe. There was no tension in the air when we came home. Nobody was measuring the atmosphere at the door. Dinner was just dinner. Evening was just evening. The ordinary rhythm of a day was allowed to be ordinary, without the constant background threat that turns ordinary moments into small acts of survival.

I was in preschool in the mornings. Walking there and back. Learning the social architecture of small children in a structured environment... how to share, how to navigate conflict without it becoming catastrophic, how to exist alongside people without constantly monitoring them for signs of danger.

I was in the gym in the evenings sometimes. Learning the beginning of something that would become the central thread of my adult life. Learning to fall and get up. Learning that discomfort is not the same as danger. Learning that a body pushed past its comfort zone is capable of things the untested body cannot imagine.

And I was watching Rob.

That ongoing education might have been the most important one. Because what I was learning in the gym was a craft. But what I was learning from watching Rob was something more foundational. I was learning what a man could look like. What presence without threat felt like. What it meant to be strong without making the people around you pay for it.

He was not perfect. Nobody is. And I am not trying to construct a mythology out of a man who was human. But he was consistent. And consistency, in my experience, is the rarest and most underrated quality a person can bring to a child's life. Not the grand gestures. Not the dramatic moments of intervention or inspiration.

Just showing up the same way tomorrow as you did today.

That was new. That was something I had never had before. And it was, as it turns out, exactly what I needed more than anything else.

. . .

Kintsugi

There is a Japanese art form called kintsugi.

The word translates roughly to golden joinery. The practice involves repairing broken pottery not by hiding the cracks or making them invisible, but by filling them with gold... lacquer mixed with powdered precious metal... so that the repaired piece is, in some ways, more beautiful for having been broken. The fractures become the feature. The history of damage becomes part of the aesthetic.

The philosophy underneath the practice is the part that has stayed with me.

It is the idea that the history of a thing... including its damage, including the moments when it came apart... is not something to be erased or concealed. It is something to be honored. To be worked with. The crack in the bowl is not a failure. It is evidence of a history. And a history, properly understood, can become the most beautiful thing about something.

I did not know about kintsugi when I was four years old, walking into a small gym in a small town in Ohio for the first time.

But what was happening to me was something in that direction.

Rob was not trying to fix what had been broken. He was not trying to erase the years in that trailer or make it as though they hadn't happened. He couldn't do that. Nobody could. What he was doing, without necessarily having a philosophy or a framework for it, was something simpler and more powerful: he was looking at a small boy who had cracks running through him and deciding that those cracks were not the final word. That they were not evidence of permanent damage. That they were, in fact, places where something new could be poured in.

He poured in control. Purpose. A model of strength that did not require a victim. A sense that the body could be an instrument of dignity rather than a site of helplessness.

And the Sensei poured in something else: the belief that effort is its own reward. That showing up and working hard and being present in the attempt is not nothing. It is the whole thing. That discipline is not punishment but the path to something you are trying to become.

I was cracked. I am cracked still, in ways that have simply become part of the architecture of who I am.

But the cracks were being filled.

Not closed. Filled.

There is a difference. Closing a crack means pretending it wasn't there. Filling it means acknowledging it, working with it, letting something come in through the opening that wouldn't have had a way in if the surface had remained unbroken.

I was four years old, and for the first time, someone was teaching me that the places where I had been broken were not something to be hidden.

They were the thing that let the light in.

. . .

The Bright Side

I want to pause here before we move forward into the harder chapters that are still ahead.

Because this one is different from the ones that came before it. The first four chapters of this story are built out of a particular kind of material... darkness, violence, the long shadow that those years cast over everything that followed. They are true. They are necessary. You cannot understand where I ended up without understanding where I started.

But this chapter is built out of something else.

This chapter is what the light looks like when it starts to come back.

And I want to be honest about what that looked like, because I think a lot of people who have been through the kind of early years I described in the first four chapters have a complicated relationship with the good things that eventually arrived. Not because the good things weren't real. But because there is a particular pattern of thinking that forms inside a difficult childhood, a way of waiting for things to turn, that makes it hard to simply receive what is being offered without looking for the catch.

When you grow up in an environment where kindness was often a transaction and warmth was often a prelude to something else, you learn to be suspicious of both. You learn to read the gift for what it might be concealing. You learn to enjoy the candy while part of you is already bracing for what comes next.

That habit doesn't disappear just because the circumstances change.

I was receiving something genuinely good during this period. Rob, who showed up the same way every day. A gym. A home where the air was breathable. A mother beginning to find her footing. A Sensei whose voice told me I was capable of more.

And some part of me, even then, was waiting for it to break.

It didn't.

Not all at once. Not immediately. There were harder chapters ahead, and we will get to them. But what I needed to learn... what this season was teaching me, even if I was too young to receive the full lesson... was that some things are simply what they appear to be. That a person who shows up consistently and treats you with respect is not necessarily building toward something they will eventually take away. That not every gift has strings. That not every kindness is a transaction.

That understanding took years to fully arrive.

But it started here.

In a small gym in a small town in Ohio. With a borrowed confidence. With a Sensei's voice telling me I could do more than I thought. With

Rob sitting across from me asking a question that assumed I had control over what came next.

You are going to encounter people in your life who pour gold into your cracks.

They may not look the way you expect. They may not arrive the way you imagined. They may come through a chance meeting... a school friend who became a stepfather, a VHS tape on a Tuesday evening, a gym that smelled like ambition and worn floors.

But they are real. And what they offer is real.

The question is whether you are willing to receive it.

A lot of us who grew up inside dysfunction have difficulty with that. We are so accustomed to the catch that we can't take the gift at face value. We are so practiced at bracing that we can't simply open. We hold the gold at arm's length because the last thing that looked like gold was actually leverage.

But here is what I have learned, and what this chapter is built around:

Borrowed belief is still belief.

When someone offers you their confidence in you... when they see something in you that you cannot yet see in yourself, when they hold a version of you that is larger and more capable than the one you are currently inhabiting... you do not have to have earned it yet to receive it. You do not have to have proof. You do not have to fully believe it yourself before you let it in.

You can borrow it.

You can operate on the scaffolding of someone else's faith in you while your own is still forming. You can let their vision of who you could become serve as the north star while you work your way toward it. And then, over time, as you show yourself through effort and discipline and showing up what you are actually capable of... the borrowed belief becomes your own.

That is what happened to me in that gym.

And that is what I spent the next several decades trying to pay forward.

The Sensei who used his voice to build something in me instead of take something from me became the blueprint for the instructor I would eventually become. The version of strength I first glimpsed in that grainy recording became the version of strength I have tried to model in my own schools, with my own students, in every room where I have had the privilege of someone's attention.

Not strength as dominance.

Not power as the ability to make others afraid.

Strength as steadiness. Power as presence. The kind of force that lifts rather than levels.

That blueprint was given to me when I was four years old, by a man who sat me down after I lost my favorite toy and asked a question that assumed I had a choice.

I did not know then what a gift that was.

I know now.

And if there is anyone reading this who is waiting for permission to receive what is genuinely being offered to them... someone who is holding the gold at arm's length because everything in their history says to check for the strings first... let me offer you this:

Some people are the real thing.

Some gifts are just gifts.

Some voices are building you, not using you.

Let them.

Let the gold in through the cracks.

That is where the light comes from.

And you have been in the dark long enough.

. . .

NUMBNESS ISN'T HEALING ... GET HELP FOR THE OPEN WOUND

...

Some nightmares loosen their grip.

They don't let go.

That is the thing no one warns you about on the other side of escape. You imagine, if you survive long enough to imagine anything, that distance will do the work. That once the source of the damage is behind you, the damage follows it. That the body, given safety, will simply ... exhale. Reset. Return to some version of before.

It doesn't work that way.

The nervous system does not care about geography. It does not check the new address or register the absence of the threat. It keeps the record exactly as it was written ... in the flinch at a certain tone of voice, in the hypervigilance that fills a room before a door opens, in the particular way a person goes somewhere else entirely when the quiet gets too quiet and there is nothing left between them and the thing they have been running from.

My mother had escaped the man.

She had not escaped what he left inside her.

And for years ... while life, on the surface, was assembling itself into something that looked like normal ... that is the story that was actually happening underneath.

. . .

A Quiet House in a Small Town

Things grew with Rob the way real things grow. Not dramatically. Not with announcement. Just steadily, the way trust accumulates between people who keep showing up the same way.

He married her.

We moved into a house in a small town in northeast Ohio. Quiet streets. Predictable rhythms. The kind of place where the neighbors knew your name and the seasons announced themselves without ambiguity and nothing about the exterior of your life suggested anything other than ordinary.

On the surface, things were right. And in many ways, they were.

Rob was a good man. Consistent. Steady in the way I had come to understand steadiness as the most reliable measure of a person's character. He worked. He showed up. He did not bring the wrong kind of weather into a room. He was present without being loud, involved without being intrusive. He was building something with us, and he meant it.

But even he could see it. I think he saw it clearly and early ... that the damage in my mother ran deeper than he could reach. He could love her. He could stay. He could create the kind of stable container that gives a wounded person the best possible conditions to heal. But he could not do the healing. Nobody can do that for someone else.

The days were fine. Routines, school, dinner, the ordinary forward motion of a family living inside a predictable week.

But when the dark came ... so did the nightmares.

And she needed something to stand between herself and them.

. . .

What the Era Made Possible

This is the part where the world my mother was living in becomes part of the story.

Seeking help was not a mainstream thing. It was not something you did and came back from without a mark on you. If you went to see a psychiatrist, the translation was simple and brutal: you were crazy. If you admitted you were struggling after leaving an abusive relationship, the quiet implication was that you should be grateful you got out. What more do you want? Move on.

Adding weight to an already-heavy load.

And if you admitted you were drinking to cope ... well. That carried its own label. Not survivor. Not someone who needed help. Drunk. Weak. Unable to handle what life handed her.

Those labels were heavier than the bottle.

So she didn't ask for help. Not for a long time. Because asking for help required walking into a system that was almost certain to shame her for needing it. And she had already endured enough shame to last several lifetimes.

She did what the options available to her made possible.

She drank.

. . .

The Can Tabs

There was a contest at school. The kind of thing teachers do to make a mundane goal feel like a competition ... collect the most aluminum can tabs and win a prize. A free pizza at Pizza Hut. I was in.

I showed up with more tabs than anyone in the class.

Not even close.

The teacher looked at the pile I dumped on her desk and then looked at me. She asked how I had gotten so many.

I told her the truth the way only a child can tell the truth ... completely, without filters, without any awareness of what the answer might reveal. They came from the beer cans, I said. The ones on the counter.

I remember her face changing.

I did not understand why. I had answered honestly. I had won the contest. I had a free pizza coming. The cans were always there, so there were always tabs, and I had been saving them for weeks because I had a goal and the resource was available and that seemed like reasonable logic to me.

That was the first moment, I think, that I registered something was off. Not because of what I'd said. Because of what her face said back.

It was concern. A specific, quiet, adult concern that a child feels without being able to name. The kind that means: this child has told me something without knowing he told me anything at all.

I walked away with my pizza coupon and filed the moment. The way I had learned to file things. Put it somewhere below where it could be looked at directly and keep moving.

But it stayed.

. . .

What I Came Home To

She would come home from work and the shift would begin.

Not unwinding. Not the kind of drink at the end of a day that is about relaxing. This was escaping. There is a difference, and even as a child I understood it on some level, even without the language for it. Unwinding moves toward presence. Escaping moves away from it. Her eyes would be somewhere I couldn't follow. The television would run ... soap operas, usually. Other people's manufactured drama, loud enough to fill the room, simple enough to require nothing.

By the time I got home from school, she was often already well on her way.

Milwaukee's Best. The cans on the counter, sometimes a row of them, sometimes more. That smell is embedded in those years for me in a way I cannot separate from them. Flat, dense, specific. I catch it now on a warm night walking past a bar and something in me tightens before I've consciously registered why. The body keeps the record.

Friends would come over sometimes and ask questions. Why does your mom drink so much? I didn't have a framework for the question. I thought it was just what people did. It was so constant, so much the texture of ordinary life as I understood it, that the idea of it being unusual hadn't fully formed yet.

Eventually I stopped inviting people over.

Not because I made a conscious decision about it. More like I slowly stopped suggesting it, stopped mentioning it, found other places to be when other kids were gathering. The management of it got easier when there was no one around who might notice what I had stopped being able to see.

. . .

The Bedroom We Turned Into a Gym

Rob was handy in the way that men of a certain generation are handy ... capable with tools, comfortable with projects, the kind of person who sees a problem in physical space and knows what to do with it.

He converted a bedroom.

Took the furniture out, put the right equipment in, and gave me somewhere to go when the rest of the house had nothing useful to offer. A training room. Small, functional, smelling of rubber mat and effort. A room with a purpose.

He would come in and teach me things. Techniques. Fundamentals. The kind of patient, methodical instruction that does not require a dojo to be real. Just a person who knows something and a kid who is willing to learn and enough space to move.

I trained.

When she was on the couch somewhere I couldn't reach her, I trained. When the eyes were absent and the television was running and the counter told the story of what the afternoon had already been ... I went to that room and I worked. I found in the movement something I could not find anywhere else in that house during those hours. A thing to focus on. A direction. A self that existed separate from the circumstances surrounding it.

I was building something, even then. I didn't have a name for it. I just knew that the room with the mat was better than the room with the couch, and so that is where I went.

Rob showed up for me in that room in ways I don't think either of us would have articulated at the time. He was still trying to reach her. And when he couldn't ... when the wound was deeper than he had access to ... he poured what he had into me instead.

I received it.

· · ·

The Pattern I Didn't Know Was a Pattern

My mornings ran on their own clock.

Rob and my mother would already be gone by the time I needed to be moving. Work had its own schedule. So I learned to run mine. Set my own alarm. Make whatever was available for breakfast. Get myself out the door.

Come home to whatever the afternoon had become.

Fix something to eat. Go to the room. Train. Move through the evening inside whatever version of quiet the house offered that night.

That was the pattern. And I did not understand it as a pattern at the time ... did not understand that what I was doing, day after day, was raising myself inside the architecture of someone else's unhealed wound. I understood it as just life. Tuesday looks like this. Wednesday looks like this. You adapt to the shape of what you're given because you do not have the frame of reference to know it could be shaped differently.

Children are extraordinarily adaptable. That is not a compliment. It is a survival mechanism.

And the thing about survival mechanisms is that they work. Right up until they don't. Right up until you are old enough to look back at what you normalized and understand, for the first time, what you were actually living inside.

I was a kid making my own dinner while my mother was gone somewhere the bottle had taken her.

I did not know that wasn't right.

I just knew how to manage it.

. . .

The War That Never Got an Ending

Every night, when the work day ended and the noise of the house settled and there was nothing left to stand between her and the quiet ... she was back in that room.

The headboard. The extended arm. The gun. The flinch that had become muscle memory. The particular terror of a person who has learned, at the cellular level, that the space she occupies is not guaranteed to be safe.

Trauma does not care about geography. It does not check the new address. It does not register the absence of the person who caused it. It lives in the nervous system, and the nervous system keeps its own clock, running on its own time, unbothered by the fact that the external situation has changed.

She had married a good man. She lived in a quiet house. Nobody was going to hurt her.

Her body did not know that yet.

The bottle made the nights quieter. It blurred the edges of the images that wouldn't stop coming. It created a kind of artificial mercy between her and the things that visited without permission. I understand that now in a way I couldn't as a child. I understand what it was paying for, or trying to pay for.

It was not weakness.

It was a woman trying to survive a war with the only weapon available to her.

The tragedy is not that she reached for it.

The tragedy is that no one handed her something better.

. . .

The Attempts

She tried.

I want to say that clearly because it is true and it matters. She was not a person who had decided this was as far as she was going. She tried. She went to AA meetings. She would come home from them different … not fixed, but lighter somehow. Like she had been in a room where the truth of her situation was allowed to exist without shame, and the relief of that was its own kind of oxygen.

I would watch her in those periods the way a child watches who has been disappointed before. With hope. The guarded kind. The kind that has learned not to fully open because fully open costs too much when the thing you hoped for doesn't hold.

It didn't always hold.

I know she went to at least one meeting drunk.

I know because I remember what happened on the way there. A half mile down the road she hit a telephone pole. The car, the pole, the call … I don't remember the exact sequence of how I found out. I just remember knowing. And I remember the particular way that knowledge settled in me ... not with shock, because shock requires something to be unexpected, and by then nothing quite was.

Just another layer added to what I was already carrying.

Each time she tried and it didn't stick, something in me recalibrated. The hope didn't disappear all at once. It just ... adjusted downward. Quietly. The way a dial turns so slowly you don't notice it moving until you look up and realize you're somewhere different than where you started.

I stopped expecting the change and started just hoping for the attempt.

And then I stopped expecting that too.

. . .

What It Cost

Untreated trauma has a cost. Not just for the person carrying it. For everyone in proximity to it.

Rob had tried. Quietly, consistently, in the way that was his nature. He had stayed when staying cost him something. He had built the gym. He had shown up for me in the space between what he could reach in her and what I needed from someone. He had loved her through things that most people would have left over years before he did.

But hope erodes. Even in good men. Even in patient ones.

The attempts that didn't hold, the nights that looked the same as the nights before them, the particular helplessness of watching someone you love disappear into something you cannot follow them into and cannot pull them out of ... it accumulated. The way everything accumulates eventually. Past the point where love alone can carry it.

They grew apart.

Not in a dramatic way. Not with a single moment that defined the end of it. Just the slow separation that happens when two people have been living in the same house for long enough that the house itself becomes the only thing they still share. They were in the same space. They were not in the same life anymore.

My mother started to self-sabotage. I don't think she would have used that word. I'm not sure she had the framework for it at the time. But looking back, I can see the pattern. When hope starts to fade, sometimes people stop fighting for the thing they're losing and start accelerating toward the loss instead. Like they need to control the ending, even if the ending is bad, because uncertainty is its own kind of unbearable.

She started seeing someone from work.

His name was Dave. He was a decent man ... kind, uncomplicated, nothing threatening about him. And it was understood, in the quiet way that things get understood in a marriage that has been done for a while before the paperwork catches up, that this was happening. Rob knew. The house knew. Everyone was living inside it without quite naming it out loud.

They were in the same house and they were separated. For a long time.

I don't think Rob wanted to fight for it by the end. I don't think he had anything left to fight with. He had given what he had. It wasn't enough to reach the place where the wound actually lived. And I don't think he blamed himself for that. Some wounds are simply not reachable from the outside, no matter how much the person on the outside wants to help.

He just ... let it go.

And with that, a version of stability I had built my footing on let go too.

. . .

The Other Thing I Watched

While my mother was cycling through the same patterns, Rob quietly did something I did not fully understand at the time.

He quit drinking.

He quit smoking too.

No announcement. No dramatic declaration. He just stopped. The man who had been present through all of it, who had watched the erosion up close and absorbed his share of what it cost ... decided at some point that he was going in a different direction. And then he went.

I was a kid. I did not have the language to name what I was watching or the perspective to understand its significance. I filed it the way I filed most things in those years. Somewhere below the surface, beneath the daily management of whatever the house required.

But it stayed.

There is a thing that happens sometimes in hard environments that nobody talks about enough. You learn not only from what people show you to do, but from what they show you not to do. The negative blueprint. The clear picture of a direction you do not want to go, drawn so specifically and so consistently that it works like a map in reverse. You know where that road leads because you have watched someone walk it. And something in you, some quiet and self-preserving part, files the information and makes a decision you won't consciously recognize for years.

I didn't know it then. I had no framework for it.

But watching Rob choose differently, quietly, without fanfare, while everything around him was pulling toward the familiar pull of numbing ... that planted something. A seed that would not surface fully until later. A path I could not yet see but was already, somewhere underneath, beginning to walk toward.

Sometimes the most important lessons we receive are the ones we don't know we're learning.

. . .

Bunk Beds

Before it was fully over, my mother moved into my room.

We got bunk beds.

There is something I have never fully known how to describe about that arrangement. Sharing a room with your mother. The specific oddness of it, the way it did not fit any category of normal I had encountered. She wasn't there because we were camping or because of some temporary disruption. She was there because the marriage had collapsed inward and the room had become its own kind of shelter from the arguing, from the pressure of two people trying to occupy the same space after the thing holding them together had gone.

Her room had become a bottle of its own kind. Mine became something else.

I didn't ask questions. I moved over. Made room. That was what I knew how to do. The adaptation that a child learns so thoroughly it stops feeling like adaptation and starts feeling like just ... how you are.

I lay in the top bunk some nights listening to her breathe below me and tried to figure out what I was feeling. It wasn't anger, exactly. It wasn't resentment. It was something more like a low-grade sorrow that had been running for so long it had become indistinguishable from the background of everything else.

She was my mother. I loved her. I would have done anything for her.

And there was nothing I could do.

That is the sentence that has lived with me longer than any other from those years.

There was nothing I could do.

They divorced not long after.

It wasn't a war. There was no final explosion, no courtroom drama, no one side against the other. It was more like a slow exhale. Two people who had tried, and run out of what trying required, and finally let go of the shape of a life that had stopped working for either of them.

Rob was gone. That version of home was gone. And with it, the training room, the steady presence, the man who had shown me ... quietly, without ever naming it ... what a good man was supposed to look like.

I noticed that loss. I didn't say it out loud. I just noticed it the way you notice something essential that has been removed from a room, when you can't immediately name what's missing but the space feels wrong.

. . .

Back to the Beginning

We eventually moved back in with my grandparents.

Full circle, in the way that hard seasons sometimes close. The same harbor that had held us the first time we needed it opened again. The same quiet. The same house where the air didn't change when a car pulled into the driveway.

I was grateful for it. I think she was too, in whatever way she was capable of being grateful for things at that point. The exhaustion of the years had done something to her that I could see but couldn't name. She was still my mother. Still brave in the specific, stubborn way that was hers. Still fighting, even if the fight looked different than it had.

But the cost of untreated trauma had been running for years by then.

And it had taken things. Real things. A marriage. A home. The particular version of Rob and our family that could have been. The version of herself she might have become if someone had handed her the right tools at the right time.

None of that came back.

You don't get those years back.

That is the truest and hardest thing I know about what happens when pain goes unanswered for long enough.

It doesn't just cost the person carrying it.

It costs everything they were trying to build.

. . .

The Labels That Kept Her From Help

I have spent a long time thinking about why she didn't get the professional help she needed sooner. Part of it was access. Part of it was resources. Part of it was an era that had not yet built the infrastructure we take for granted now.

But the biggest part was the labels.

In the world my mother was navigating, the labels available to a woman who admitted she was struggling were not healing labels. They were wounding ones.

Crazy. Weak. Drunk. Can't handle her own life.

The act of asking for help required her to walk into a room and accept whatever label came with that admission. And she had already been labeled enough. She had already been made small enough by enough people in enough rooms that the prospect of doing it voluntarily, of handing someone the evidence of her struggles and waiting to see how they'd use it against her ... that was not a risk that felt survivable.

So she stayed inside the thing that was destroying her because getting out required something that felt even more dangerous.

That is not weakness.

That is what happens when the available options are all forms of loss.

And I want to name that clearly, because there are people reading this right now who are making the same calculation. Who are sitting inside something that is costing them everything, and telling themselves that asking for help would cost them something too. Their privacy. Their dignity. The story they've told themselves about who they are.

The voice that says getting help means you're broken is lying to you.

Staying untreated is what keeps you there.

. . .

The Bright Side

My mother passed in November of 2024.

I miss her every day. In the particular, specific way that you miss someone who was complicated and brave and flawed and yours. In the way that grief does not resolve but simply becomes part of the architecture of how you move through the world.

She fought for a long time. Longer and harder than most people will ever know. And the fact that she did not get the help she needed early enough to change the arc of those years is not her failure.

It is a failure of the world she lived in.

That world has changed.

Not entirely. Not perfectly. The stigma around mental health and recovery has not disappeared. There are still communities where asking for help carries a cost. There are still people navigating the same calculation my mother navigated, and arriving at the same conclusion she did, because the available options have not evolved fast enough.

But they have evolved. And they are evolving still.

The infrastructure that did not exist for my mother exists now. Teletherapy that meets you where you are. Recovery programs built around trauma-informed care. Clinical psychologists who understand that addiction is not a moral failing but a predictable response to pain that was never treated. Hotlines that are answered by people trained to meet you in crisis without judgment. Groups that gather in church basements and in online forums and in living rooms and in the specific quiet spaces where people who are carrying too much finally get to set it down in front of witnesses who understand.

You do not have to do this alone.

I want to say that again, slower.

You do not have to do this alone.

Whatever nightmare you are carrying. Whatever version of that trailer lives inside you and visits without permission in the dark. Whatever thing you have been filing and burying and carrying underground because the visible weight of it felt like more than the world would allow … there are people equipped for exactly this. Trained for it. Choosing it as their life's work because they understand what is at stake when a person does not get the help they need.

They are not waiting to judge you.

They are waiting to help.

The answer was never at the bottom of a bottle. The answer was never in a morning that begins before you've fully woken up and a counter full of evidence that last night did not go the way you needed it to go. The answer is not in the numbing, however effective the numbing feels in the short term.

The numbing just delays the wound.

And the wound, untended, gets worse.

My mother's courage was real. Her trying was real. The 30-day chips were real and the AA meetings were real and the mornings she woke up and made the choice to attempt another day were real. All of it was real and all of it mattered.

And I wish with everything in me that she had found ... earlier, more consistently, with more support around her ... the professional help that could have met the wound at its source.

Not the symptom. The source.

She deserved that.

You deserve that.

Whatever nightmares you cannot wake from, there are people equipped with the tools and the training and the perspective to help you through them. You are not asking too much. You are not too broken. You are not too far gone. You are not the exception to what recovery makes possible.

You are exactly who this is for.

My mother spent years trapped inside a prison that had no walls. She escaped the trailer but could not outrun what it had put inside her. And the world she lived in did not hand her the key.

But the world you are living in has the key.

Reach for it.

. . .

If You Need Help ... Here Is Where to Start

My mother did not have this list. The infrastructure for it barely existed in her era, and what did exist came wrapped in enough stigma that reaching for it felt like a risk she couldn't afford.

You have it. Right now. In your hand or on your screen.

These are real resources. Free, confidential, and staffed by people who are not there to judge you ... only to help you find the next right step. You do not have to have it figured out before you call. You do not have to know exactly what you need. You just have to make the call.

If you or someone you love is struggling with alcohol, addiction, or the kind of untreated pain that drives both ... start here.

SAMHSA National Helpline | 1-800-662-4357 | samhsa.gov

> Free, confidential, 24/7. English and Spanish. Substance use and mental health referrals for individuals and families. Text your ZIP code to 435748 to find local resources.

988 Suicide & Crisis Lifeline | Call or text 988

> For anyone in emotional distress or crisis. Not only for suicide ... if the weight is too heavy right now, this line is for you.

Crisis Text Line | Text HOME to 741741

> Free, 24/7. If calling feels like too much right now, texting is enough. A trained crisis counselor will be on the other end.

Al-Anon / Alateen | 1-800-356-9996 | al-anon.org

> For the people who love someone struggling with alcohol. If you grew up in a home like mine, or if someone you love is in one right now … this line exists for you, not just for them.

NAMI Helpline | 1-800-950-6264 | nami.org

> National Alliance on Mental Illness. Peer support, practical resources, and next steps for people living with mental health conditions and their families.

FindTreatment.gov | findtreatment.gov

> SAMHSA's treatment locator. Enter your location and find nearby facilities, programs, and providers.

National Association for Children of Alcoholics | 1-888-554-2627

> If you grew up in a home shaped by a parent's drinking and you are still carrying the weight of those years … this line exists for you specifically.

These numbers exist because the people who built them understand something essential: asking for help is not the end of your story. It is where the better part of it begins.

The answers are never at the bottom of a bottle.

But they are at the other end of a phone call.

. . .

CHAPTER SEVEN

FACE THE GHOST
OR LIVE HAUNTED

We didn't stay at my grandparents' long.

I think I understand why now, in a way I couldn't then. My grandparents loved her. They would have kept us indefinitely. But they would also have noticed. That's the thing about people who know you well and love you honestly ... they see what you are working to keep invisible. And my mother was not ready to be seen. Not yet. Not that clearly.

So we found an apartment close enough that you could throw a stone from the front door and probably hit their house. Near enough for comfort. Far enough for privacy. And we moved in with Dave.

. . .

Dave

Dave was already part of the picture by then. Had been for a while. My mother hadn't arrived at him the way you arrive at a new chapter ... she had been building toward him quietly, the way people do when the official story and the actual story have come slightly apart from each other.

He was a different kind of man than Rob had been.

Rob gave me roots. He showed me that I didn't have to be a victim of my circumstances. That the choices in front of me were real choices. That a man could walk into a room without making it dangerous. That strength and volume were not the same thing. Those were foundational gifts. The kind you build everything else on.

Dave gave me something different. He gave me wings.

He was what I would call ... and I mean this with genuine respect and affection ... a nerd. The consummate kind. The kind for whom technology was not a tool but a lens. A way of seeing the world as a set of systems that could be understood, improved, and built. He thought about how things worked. He thought about what was possible when you understood the mechanics underneath the surface. And he was genuinely, quietly excited about the future in a way I had not encountered before.

He didn't announce any of this. He just ... lived it.

The kitchen table in that apartment was part desk, part workbench, part laboratory. Components and cables and the quiet hum of machines that were always in some state of being assembled or taken apart. That was his natural habitat. And without making a lesson of it, without sitting me down and explaining what he was trying to give me ... he started giving it.

· · ·

Thirteen Hours

I watched him one afternoon, puttering around on his computer. The way he moved through it. Purposeful. At home inside the logic of the thing.

I said something like: I want a computer.

He looked up. There was a beat, the kind that precedes a decision rather than a response. A small smirk.

He said: alright.

He pointed to a book on the table. Said it would tell me everything I needed to know about how to build one. Then he pointed to the collection of components sitting next to it … a motherboard, a processor, drives, cables, a case. Everything required. Already there. Already waiting.

Have at it, he said.

And then he left me to it.

Thirteen hours later, I had a computer. Not a working one quite yet … there were a couple of jumper settings I had to come back to him for, small technical details I hadn't been able to puzzle out from the book alone. But I had built it. I understood how all of it went together. I knew which piece connected to which, and why, and what each one was responsible for. I had gone from someone who wanted a thing to someone who could build the thing.

That lesson was not about computers.

Rob had taught me I could control my circumstances. That I wasn't a passenger in my own life, that the choices in front of me were real and mine to make. Dave was teaching me something adjacent but distinct. He was teaching me that everything I would ever need to build the future I wanted was already available to me ... that the limit was not access or permission or the right circumstances. The limit was willingness. The willingness to pick up the book. To sit with the confusion until it resolved. To build the thing yourself rather than wait for someone to hand it to you ready-made.

What you need is right between your ears, if you have the will to learn.

That is not a small thing to hand a kid. Especially a kid who had spent a significant portion of his life learning that the adults in the room were not reliably in control of what happened next. Dave was showing me that I could be the exception to that. That I could be the adult in the room, for myself, if I was willing to do the work.

I loved him for that. I still do.

. . .

The New Shape of Things

The pattern of those days was familiar in its bones, even in a new place.

I kept training. By this point, martial arts had stopped being the thing Rob had introduced me to and had become the thing that was mine. I was competing. Traveling. Measuring myself against kids from other gyms, other states, other backgrounds. The mat is indifferent to your history. It only cares what you do with what you have in the moment. That indifference, which might have felt cold, felt like relief. A level surface. No extra weight carried for things that happened before the match.

I was building something. A reputation, small but accumulating. A sense of myself that existed independent of the apartment and whatever the evenings looked like when I got home.

Because some things hadn't changed.

The drinking was still there. Heavier, if anything. Dave drank too, which gave the two of them a kind of shared frequency … a way of being in the same orbit that didn't require explanation. The cans stacked on the kitchen counter. Fruit flies hovering in that particular way they do when something has been left too long, when the rot has been ignored past the point of easy management. The apartment carried the smell of it. Not dramatically. Just … constantly. A low note underneath everything else.

I recognized it. I had grown up with it. What I was developing, slowly, was the frame of reference to understand it as something specific rather than just … life. I was spending more time outside. With friends. My feet and my bike could take me most places I needed to go, and I used that. I moved through the neighborhood. I was in other people's houses. I was watching other versions of how a day could be assembled.

And I was starting to notice what was different.

Not with anger yet. With something quieter. The early edge of a question that didn't fully arrive for years: what is this, exactly? And what does something else look like?

The wound was still open in that apartment. The cans were the evidence of it. But life, oddly, was also good. Not in spite of the contradiction. Inside it. Both things occupying the same space, the way they tend to in real lives that don't have clean narratives. The training was real. Dave's gift was real. My mother's love was real. And the festering on the kitchen counter was real.

All of it, at once.

I was learning to hold all of it at once.

. . .

The Phone Call

I was sixteen when my aunt called.

My father's sister. From his side of the family. The side that had been, for as long as I could remember, a set of names and faces attached to nothing. People who existed in the abstract, the way history exists before it becomes something you've touched. I knew I had an aunt. I knew there was a grandmother. I knew, somewhere beyond the trailer and the violence and the years of silence, there were people connected to him by blood and therefore connected to me in some technical sense. But the connection had never had texture.

She told me my grandmother had passed.

My father's mother. My grandmother. The woman I had glimpses of from before we left ... a crib, prayers before bed, the impressionistic fragments that survive from that age when memory is still forming its filing system. She had been real in some part of me, even without a relationship to anchor her. And she was gone.

I was sad in the specific way you grieve a relationship that never fully got to be one. Not for the person you lost, exactly ... for the version of the relationship that died before it was ever built. The sadness of an absence that had always been an absence, finally given a name.

My aunt asked if my father could reach out. If we could all come together. A memorial. A gathering of the family I had never known.

My mother left it to me. That was who she was. Even when the decision had to cost her something, even when I could feel the alarm bells running underneath her steady voice, she handed it to me. Your choice. Your life. Your call to make.

I thought about it.

. . .

The Plan I Had

I am going to be honest about what I was planning.

Years of training. A body that had been built for competition. Testosterone and sixteen and every night those walls had held and every morning the counter had told its story. The grief of a boy who had watched his mother survive something she should never have had to survive, and filed the anger from all of it in a place he had not yet figured out how to open.

I had a plan for when he walked through the door.

It wasn't complicated. It didn't require much thought. He would arrive, and I would make years of stored frustration into something physical, something immediate, something that would finally balance a ledger that had been running in the wrong direction for as long as I could remember. I was not going to fight him out of rage. I was going to fight him out of a cold, clear conviction that this was the most honest response available.

I told myself it was justice.

Part of me believed it.

I spent weeks inside that anticipation. The slow build of knowing something is coming ... the way a storm looks on a forecast before it arrives, the particular kind of dread and readiness that lives in the body when you know a confrontation is coming and you have decided not to run from it. I woke up with it. I trained with it. I lay in bed at night and rehearsed.

The buzz of the intercom. The sound of his voice. The door opening. The moment.

I had lived inside that sequence a hundred times before he ever showed up.

. . .

What Actually Happened

He buzzed from downstairs.

I pressed the intercom. Asked who was there. And I heard his voice for the first time in years on the other end of that small speaker ... older than I remembered it, or maybe I was just old enough now to hear it differently. Either way, it landed.

I buzzed him in.

I stood at the door while he made his way up to the third floor. My body was doing what a trained body does when it is preparing for something

... the particular readiness that martial arts builds in you, the way your awareness narrows and sharpens and goes very quiet. I had rehearsed this. I knew exactly what I was going to do.

He knocked.

I opened the door.

And I did not hit him.

Our eyes met, and something happened that I was not prepared for. All those weeks of rehearsal, all that certainty, all the clarity of a plan built out of years of legitimate grievance ... and none of it survived the moment his eyes found mine. Because what I saw in his face was not the monster. What I saw was a man. Smaller than I had built him in my memory. Older. Carrying something I didn't have a word for yet but recognized immediately in the way you recognize familiar weight.

I hugged him.

Not a polite hug. Not the careful, arms-length contact of two people who are supposed to be performing something. The kind of hug that lasts. The kind that lingers because the body is saying something the words haven't caught up to yet. He held me back. His arms were around me and I could feel in them something I had not expected to feel ... remorse. Real remorse. The weight of years of absence packed into a single moment of contact.

For that moment, he was my father.

Not the man from the trailer. Not the silhouette at the door. Not the Zippo lighter and the back turned on two people who needed him. Just ... my father. The one I had wanted him to be. The one who put me up on the bar at the VFW and grinned like he'd built me himself. The one who handed me Necco Wafers in the fluorescent light of a gas station and meant something by it, even if the meaning was complicated.

For that moment, both things were true at once.

. . .

The Family I Didn't Know

We went to the memorial. My mother, my father, and me, in that same van, though this time my seat was considerably more comfortable.

I could feel her apprehension. I had learned, over years of proximity, to read my mother's body the way you read weather. The particular quality of her stillness when she was managing something. The way she held herself when she was choosing, deliberately, to give me space for something that cost her to allow.

She was doing that. She was giving me this, at whatever it cost her, because she understood that it was mine to have.

My grandparents' house. His parents. Not the ones who had sheltered us from the storm. These were strangers to me in every way except the genetic. Aunts. An uncle. Cousins. A grandfather, the patriarch, weathered and quiet in the specific way of men who have lived long enough to understand that most things are not worth arguing about.

They had questions. About my life. About what I had been up to. About who I had become. And the questions were warm ... genuinely warm. I could feel the love in my aunts, the particular love that people carry for someone they have missed and wanted to know and been kept from by circumstances they also could not fully control. We took pictures in the backyard. I still have them.

But I never asked the questions burning inside me.

Not once. Not directly.

Where were you? Why didn't you come? Why did so many years of my life pass without you in them? I was your son. I existed. Why didn't you ask?

Those questions were there. They did not leave. I just chose, on that afternoon with the pictures and the backyard and the aunts who loved me, not to ask them out loud. I don't know exactly why. I think some part of me understood that there were no answers that would land right. That whatever he offered in response would either satisfy me in a way that felt too easy or fail me in a way that would make the afternoon impossible to recover. I let it sit.

I filed it. The way I had learned to file things.

For the time being.

. . .

The Gift

We came back to the apartment afterward. All of us. The day hadn't been bad. It had, in some ways, been more than I expected. The aunts were real. The love in that backyard had been real. And my father ... he had been present in a way I had not been prepared for. Somber at the memorial. Warm with his family. Something like the man I had caught glimpses of in those late nights at the VFW, the version of him that the world outside our trailer got to see.

He had brought me a gift.

A large box. Heavy. I held it and felt the familiar configuration of something given after something owed, the architecture of it landing in me before I even opened it. A model ship. Old-world, the kind Christopher Columbus would have sailed on. Large sails. Wooden construction. Painted with a precision and detail that told me someone had either spent a great deal of money or found it somewhere and decided it was significant enough.

I thanked him. My mother had raised me to always be respectful, and I was. I took it to my room to find a place for it.

That was when I started to hear them.

. . .

What I Heard

The voices carried down the hallway. Not raised. Not a fight. Just conversation, the specific tone of two people who have history standing in the same room and deciding what to do with it.

My mother was being gracious. That was who she was. She was thanking him. For making the effort. For coming back. For taking the time to spend with me. Thanking him … this woman who had survived what she had survived, who had pressed herself against the foundation of a trailer in a northeast Ohio winter holding her child and barely breathing while he stumbled around on the landing above them … she was thanking him.

And that is when he said it.

He told her he hadn't come back for me.

He came back for her.

I sat in my room with the model ship in my hands and I listened to those words settle into me.

The hug rewound in my mind. The linger of it. The remorse I thought I had felt in his arms. And beneath all of it, working its way through slowly, the specific devastation of understanding that the moment I had believed in ... the moment where he was my father, fully present, carrying the weight of what he had missed and meaning it ... that moment had a different story running underneath it.

He had not come back for me.

I had been a reason to show up. Not the reason.

I sat with that the way you sit with something that has just rearranged the furniture inside you. Quietly. Not with rage. With something slower and more complete.

. . .

What Happened Next

My mother's voice changed.

I had heard her voice in many registers over the years. I had heard her afraid, and exhausted, and trying, and grieving things she never fully named out loud. I had heard her be gracious in situations that did not deserve her grace.

What I heard next was different.

She told him that was never going to happen. That ship had sailed a long time ago. And then she told him ... in the particular way my mother could say something unambiguous without raising her voice ... that he didn't get to come back and do this. Not to her. Not to me.

He backpedaled. Maybe it was a poor attempt at charm. Maybe he believed that enough time had passed to rewrite the story. Whatever it was, my mother was not interested in negotiating with it.

She asked him to leave.

He huffed. He said things. He walked out the door.

And this time, when the door closed behind him ... it was different than the last time. The last time, a door closing behind him had been survival. The desperate relief of two people who had made it through something and were now catching their breath.

This time, the door closing felt like something finished.

A loop closed.

Not cleanly. Not without cost. But closed.

. . .

The Weight of What I Didn't Do

I never asked him the questions.

Not that afternoon in the backyard. Not before my mother asked him to leave. Not ever, because there was no after.

I have sat with that choice for a long time. Wondered whether I should have. Whether the questions deserved to be spoken out loud, whether the answers, whatever they would have been, would have given me something I didn't find another way.

I don't think so. Not anymore.

What I have come to understand, slowly, is that some closures don't arrive in the form you hoped for. You imagine that the conversation will be the thing. The confrontation. The moment where you finally say everything you've been carrying and the other person finally hears it and something shifts. You imagine that clarity is on the other side of that exchange.

Sometimes the clarity is what you learn when the exchange turns out to be what it actually is.

He came back for her.

That sentence closed more questions than any answer he could have offered to the ones I had been holding. It told me exactly who he was. Not the monster I had built him into. Not the father I had briefly believed in during that hug. Just a man. A flawed, limited, complicated man who had never fully understood what he had left behind ... and who, when he found a reason to walk back through that door, had walked through it carrying the wrong reason.

That is not an indictment. It is just the truth.

And the truth, even when it disappoints, is cleaner than the fantasy.

. . .

The Bright Side

Dave taught me that everything I needed was already available to me. That the limit was never access or permission or the right set of circumstances. The limit was knowledge. And the willingness to go get it.

I didn't know it at the time, but I was about to apply that lesson in a direction I never expected.

There is something nobody told me about ghosts.

You spend so much time afraid of the encounter that you forget the encounter itself is the cure.

I had carried my father as a ghost for years. Not the man ... the ghost. The version of him that lived in memory and imagination and the particular dark that arrives without warning. The silhouette in the doorway. The Zippo lighter. The back turned on two people who needed him. That ghost was enormous. It had weight and presence and it occupied real estate in me that I had never fully accounted for.

And then he rang the buzzer. And I heard his voice on the intercom. And the ghost became a man.

Not the man I wanted. Not the father the story deserved. Just a man, aging and flawed and carrying his own unexamined weight, who had come back for the wrong reason and said so out loud where his son could hear it.

That was not what I hoped for.

It was what I needed.

Because what I needed was not the reunion. What I needed was the knowledge. The specific, unambiguous, no-longer-theoretical knowledge of who he actually was, stripped of the mythology I had built up over years of absence. The ghost had no edges. The ghost could expand to fill whatever space my imagination gave it. The man had edges. The man was finite. The man was someone I could finally, after all those years, actually see.

He came back for her.

Five words. And just like that, thirteen hours of questions I had been carrying ... the why didn't you come, the where were you, the why didn't you ask about me ... they dissolved. Not because each question finally got its answer. Because one sentence made all of them irrelevant. He told me exactly who he was. And once you know who someone is, you stop needing them to explain themselves.

You can't build a computer without knowing how the pieces fit together. You can't move forward from a ghost without knowing what it actually is.

I had the knowledge now.

That was enough.

It would not be the last time I saw him. Life has its way of circling back. But those questions ... the ones I had rehearsed and never asked, the ones that had been accumulating since before I could articulate them ... they didn't have the same weight after that night. They had been answered, not in the way I had imagined, but in the only way that was ever going to be honest.

The confrontation I had planned ... the one built out of fists and years of stored frustration ... would not have given me that. It would have given me a moment. A release of pressure. And then, after the moment, the ghost would have come back, unchanged, because I had met it with force rather than with clarity.

Clarity was the thing.

The disappointment was the closure.

The ghosts that haunt us longest are the ones we never let become what they actually are. They live in the avoidance. They grow in the darkness we construct around them to keep from looking too closely. Every year you don't face them, they get a little larger. A little less specific. A little more capable of filling the whole room.

Face them when you have the chance. Not with your fists, if you can help it. With your eyes.

Get the knowledge.

The man is always smaller than the ghost.

And smaller is something you can live with.

. . .

CHAPTER EIGHT

BOUNDARIES FORGED IN FIRE GUARD THE FUTURE

The night I left, I didn't write a note.

I just packed a bag, grabbed what mattered, and walked out the door.

No speech. No dramatic exit. No final declaration of all the things I had been holding for years and never said. Just the sound of my own footsteps on the stairs and then the night air hitting my face and the quiet that follows a decision your whole body already made before your mind caught up with it.

I was done.

Not done loving her. I want to be precise about that, because the guilt that was already climbing into the car with me wanted to call it something it wasn't. I was not done loving her. I was done believing that my staying inside the fire was going to be the thing that put it out.

Some fires have to burn themselves down.

And some people have to get far enough away to stop smelling like smoke.

. . .

Years Had Passed

Let me back up. Because to understand that night, you need to understand the years that built toward it.

By the time I was in high school, I had grown into something. Not everything. Not the finished version of a person who had processed every piece of what my early childhood had handed him. But something. A self that was taking shape. A direction that was becoming clear.

Martial arts had done that. Not in some cinematic, problem-solved way. In the slow, methodical way that real discipline works. You show up. You train. You fail. You try again. You get pushed past what you thought your limit was and you find out there was more on the other side of it. Over and over. Until one day you look up and realize that the version of you who walked through that gym door for the first time... the scared, cracked, uncertain kid who had grown up measuring the temperature of every room before he walked into it... that version barely recognizes the one looking back in the mirror.

I had risen through the ranks. Put in the years. The early mornings and the sore muscles and the particular satisfaction of something clicking into place after you have worked it enough times that your body finally understands what your mind already knew. I was good. And I knew it. And for a while, I let that knowledge get ahead of me.

Showing off is a young man's tax. You pay it and you don't even know you're paying it until the bill arrives.

Mine arrived in an instant.

I don't need to make it more dramatic than it was. One moment of squandering the skill on something it wasn't built for... on performance instead of practice, on proving something instead of building something... and I was injured. The kind of injury that doesn't resolve in a few weeks. The kind that takes up residence and sets a new pace for your life whether you agreed to that pace or not. On and off my feet for the better part of a few years. Limited in the very thing that had been holding me together.

The easy move would have been to quit.

I almost made it.

My instructor talked me out of it. Not with a speech. Not with the kind of motivational address you see in movies right before the third-act comeback. He just said: come anyway. You don't have to train. Just come. Be here.

So I came.

I sat at the edge of the mat while others moved through the things I couldn't do yet. I watched. I absorbed. And because I was there, because I had showed up without the ability to perform and nothing left to prove, I started to notice something I had been moving too fast to see when I was the one drilling.

I could see what people were getting wrong before they got it wrong. I could see the moment before the mistake. I understood the mechanics from the inside in a way that the body knows but the mouth rarely finds words for... and sitting still had given me the words.

My instructor put me to work.

Not as the athlete I had been. As something I hadn't considered yet. A teacher. Someone who helped where he could, who filled the gaps, who used what he had instead of mourning what the injury had taken. I started guiding students through what I knew. Using my voice to build something in someone else the way a Sensei had once built something in me.

I did not own that school. I was a student who had stayed long enough and shown up enough to earn the right to give something back. That distinction matters. What I was doing was not mine in the sense of possession. It was mine in the sense of purpose. I had found the reason the mat had been holding me all those years.

It was never just about the fighting.

It was always about this.

. . .

A Doorway

There was a girl. My high school sweetheart. I'm not going to give her name, because this chapter isn't really about her. She was a doorway. And some of the most important people in our lives show up exactly that way... not as destinations, but as openings. As the person who walks you to the edge of something you needed to see.

What she gave me, without knowing the full weight of what she was giving, was a view I had never had before.

A family that worked.

Not a perfect family. I've come to distrust that framing the way I distrust most things that don't leave room for the human. But a family that was... present. Intact. Operating on the assumption that home was supposed to be safe. Both parents there. Both engaged. Both asking about your day because they actually wanted the answer.

I remember sitting at their dinner table for the first time. The food was warm. The conversation was easy. Her father asked me questions and listened to what I said. Her mother had the kind of warmth that doesn't announce itself... it just moves through a room quietly and makes everyone in it feel like they belong there.

I watched all of it with the careful attention of someone who had never seen this up close before. Not suspiciously. Not waiting for the catch. Just... taking it in. Filing it. Letting it reshape something in me that had been running off a different template for a long time.

This is what it can look like, I kept thinking. This is what a house feels like when nobody in it is managing the temperature.

Through that family, I started going to church. And through church, I found something I hadn't known I was searching for.

. . .

What Faith Felt Like

I'm going to try to say this accurately, because it is easy to say it wrong.

I'm not talking about religion as a system. Not a set of rules I enrolled in or a membership I obtained. What I found was something underneath all of that. Something that arrived not as an argument to be reasoned through but as a presence to be felt. A sense of being known by something that didn't flinch. That didn't leave. That had been watching the whole time and had not turned away from any of it.

If you have experienced something like that, you know exactly what I mean and no further description is necessary. If you haven't, I'm not sure language gets all the way there. What I can say is this: for a person who had grown up with the particular kind of loneliness that comes from carrying hard things alone... from having no adult in the room to tell you what was happening was wrong, to put a hand on your shoulder and say you didn't deserve this... the idea of a presence that saw everything and was not going anywhere was not small.

It was enormous.

I got baptized. I gave myself to it with the full conviction of someone who had found something real and wanted to go all the way in. The particular clean of that decision... the sense of a line being drawn, a new chapter beginning, the past acknowledged and then released into something larger... I felt it physically. Down into the places in me that had been carrying the record of everything for years.

New faith is a gift. It is also, in my experience, almost immediately challenged.

The challenge that arrived first wasn't the one I expected.

Almost as soon as I walked through the door God had opened... the relationship that had led me to it closed. She and I ended. Not dramatically. Not with a story worth telling in detail. Just the particular quiet that falls when two people have taken each other as far as they were supposed to go and it is time to go separately from here.

I was left with the faith and without the hand that had walked me to it.

Which, I would eventually understand, was exactly the point. The door was for me. The doorway was hers to be.

Other relationships came. And went. The pattern that followed those years is one I recognize now with the clarity that distance provides, though I couldn't see it clearly while I was inside it. I would get close. I would feel the pull of something real. And then something would shift, and the thing I was reaching for would slip, and I would be alone again with the familiar question that had been running underneath everything since I was old enough to ask it.

Maybe I am too broken.

Maybe I am too much.

Maybe the version of me that comes from that trailer, from those years, from that particular accumulation of things I never asked for and couldn't set down... maybe that version is not the kind that someone stays for.

I didn't have the language for what I was doing then. I do now. Some of it was circumstance. Some of it was the ordinary difficulty of young adulthood, of two people figuring out who they are and finding out they are figuring it out in different directions. But some of it... and I want to be honest about this because honesty is the whole point of this book... some of it was me. Patterns I had absorbed so early they felt like personality. A way of relating that carried the fingerprints of everything I had watched and survived. Self-sabotage wearing the costume of bad timing.

I didn't know I was doing it. That's the thing about patterns you inherit. They don't feel like patterns. They feel like just how things go.

The challenge that arrived for me came in the form of the one person I most wanted to hand this new faith to.

. . .

The Mistake New Faith Almost Always Makes

When something transforms you... when it reaches the deep places and moves things that haven't moved in years... the instinct is good. You want to offer it. You want the people you love most to have what you found. You want to walk back into the hardest rooms of your life carrying a light you didn't have before and show them what you can see now.

The instinct is right. The execution is where it goes wrong.

I carried faith like a solution. Like I had finally located the key to a lock I had been staring at my whole life and all I needed to do was explain it correctly, argue it precisely, press hard enough on the right points, and the door would open. And once the door opened, the drinking would stop. The nightmares would stop. The version of her that had been buried under years of unhealed pain would finally step into the light.

I pushed.

Hard. With all the certainty of nineteen years old and a newfound faith and a lifetime of unresolved grief about what that trauma had cost her. I wasn't being cruel. I was being desperate in the way that people are desperate when they love someone and they can see what's happening and they cannot stop it.

The harder I pushed, the harder she resisted.

I can see now what I couldn't see then. Nobody receives a gift that is being thrown at them. You cannot force someone into healing. You cannot argue someone out of their own pain. The path out of trauma is not something you can walk for someone else, no matter how clearly you can see it, no matter how much you love the person who needs to walk it.

What my pushing did was not open the door. It built a wall.

Every conversation that escalated. Every time I named what I saw with precision and watched it land as an accusation instead of an offering. Every argument that ended in silence thicker than the one before it.

I had picked up her stubbornness somewhere in the years of growing up alongside her. Two stubborn people sharing the same space, each convinced they were right, each carrying years of unresolved weight, neither one fully equipped for the conversation they were trying to have.

It was building toward something.

I just didn't know what it was going to cost to get there.

. . .

The Night That Broke

Dave had been in her life for a while by then. A good man. Patient and steady in the way that certain people are patient… not as a performance, but because their nature runs in that direction. He had seen what she was carrying and stayed anyway. He had tried to reach what most people would have recognized early on as unreachable from the outside and he had kept trying longer than most people would have.

That particular night had a weather of its own before it even started. The particular volatility that some nights carry... not building toward anything specific, just volatile from the moment the air settles after dinner. Dave was there. I was there. The conversation was already going somewhere.

And I made a choice.

Not a cruel one. Not motivated by anything darker than the accumulated frustration of years and the particular precision of someone who has been paying attention and knows exactly which argument lands. I laid it out. Carefully. The way you make a case when you believe in it.

The common denominator. Every relationship that had frayed. Every year that had cost something it shouldn't have cost. Every person who had tried and run out of what trying required. I named it without flinching: the drinking was the thing. Not a symptom of something deeper... or not only that. The thing itself. The choice that kept compounding.

Dave sat quietly. I think some part of him was relieved that someone with standing was saying it. That I could get away with the words that would have cost him something to use. He knew that. I knew that.

What I didn't calculate was how far I was from the line.

I found it anyway.

She slapped me across the face.

Not a warning. A full stop. The particular kind of slap that lands not just on your cheek but in something deeper... in the place that has been trying to hold everything together for years and has finally run out of room to absorb one more thing.

I said something back. I don't remember the exact words. I know they were designed to cut exactly as precisely as the slap had cut. I know they landed. And then I turned and walked toward my room.

She followed.

The door came between us. I tried to close it. She pushed through. I held it. And in the struggle that followed... in the moment when years of everything that had been building crested into a single physical instant... I grabbed her arm and moved her back into the hallway.

She went down.

And in the silence that followed... in the half-second before the yelling started again... something else happened.

. . .

The Voice From Before

A memory arrived. Not slowly. Immediately.

I was four years old, sitting on a couch with tears on my face and shattered plastic on the floor in front of me. A girl from the apartment building had taken my transformer... my submarine, my pocketed certainty, the thing I reached for when I needed something solid... and she had thrown it down and it had broken into pieces and I had come home with that loss sitting in my chest like a stone.

And Rob had sat across from me.

He hadn't offered comfort. He hadn't tried to patch the wound with reassurance. He had waited until I was looking at him and he had asked me a question.

Do you want this to happen again?

I was standing in that hallway, a grown man, with my mother on the floor and the silence ringing and every alarm in my nervous system going off at once... and I heard that question as clearly as if he were standing right there.

Do you want this to happen again?

And behind that question, the thing it had always carried: the assumption that I had a choice. That I was not only a thing that events happened to. That there was, inside me, a say in what came next.

I had a choice.

Even now. Even in this hallway. Even surrounded by years of everything that had led here.

I could stay. I could keep pressing. I could keep pouring what I had into a lock my key would never open. I could become, slowly and without intending to, the version of a man that I had promised at eighteen months old I would never be.

Or I could choose something different.

I chose.

I went to my room. I packed a bag. Not everything. Some clothes. The things you take when you don't know exactly how long you'll be gone but your body already knows it needs to go. I didn't leave a note. There was nothing left to say that hadn't already been said too many times in the wrong direction.

I walked out.

. . .

Where I Landed

I moved into an apartment with roommates.

Some friends. People my age who were building their own versions of the next chapter. Nobody carrying the particular weight I was carrying, or if they were, they weren't showing it, and that was fine. The point was not to find people who understood everything. The point was to find a space where the air was breathable. Where the evening was just an evening.

I want to describe what those first weeks felt like, because the contrast matters.

I had grown up learning to read rooms before I walked into them. Measuring the atmosphere. Listening for the particular quality of silence that means something is about to happen. That habit had become so automatic I had stopped noticing it was happening. It was just how I moved through the world. Carefully. Quietly. Ready.

In that apartment, I forgot to do it.

Not all at once. Gradually. The way a muscle releases when the threat it was braced for simply doesn't arrive. I would come in from training and there would be noise and food and conversation and nobody checking anyone's temperature before they spoke. Just people. Living. Ordinary and safe.

I breathed.

For the first time in a long time, I just breathed.

I kept teaching. The mat stayed constant the way it always had. The work was still there. The students showed up and the discipline showed up and the version of me that existed inside that gym was not the version that had walked out of that hallway. He was focused. He was building. He knew exactly what he was doing and why.

That clarity was not an accident. It was what the years of practice had been building toward. When everything else was uncertain, the work was certain. When the home situation was chaos, the mat was order. The discipline had been the one reliable thread running through every difficult season of my life, and it didn't fail me now.

I was not done with her. I want to be clear about that, because the guilt that arrived with me when I left kept trying to name the leaving as something final. It wasn't. I had not walked out of her life. I had walked out of the burning building. There is a difference.

But from the outside, from across the space I had finally put between us... I could start to see things I hadn't been able to see when I was standing inside them.

. . .

What Leaving Actually Was

Leaving was not abandonment.

I have needed to say that clearly to myself more than once. The guilt that comes with walking out on someone you love... especially someone who has been through what she had been through, especially a mother who had once pressed herself against a trailer foundation in the Ohio dark holding you so tightly you could feel her heartbeat... that guilt is not quiet. It is insistent. It speaks in the voice of every version of yourself that learned early that love means staying no matter what.

But I had to learn to hear a different truth underneath it.

I could not save her. Not because I hadn't tried hard enough. Not because I didn't love her enough. Because saving her was not mine to do. The wound she was carrying had been written into her before I was born, deepened by years of violence I had watched from hallways and doorframes, and the healing of it required something I didn't have available. A professional. A clinical intervention. A sustained and structured kind of help that is not something a son can provide, no matter how desperately he wants to.

I had been pouring energy into that equation for years. Watching it not add up. Watching the people around her pour their own energy in and watch it not add up. Rob. Dave. Me. All of us decent people with genuine love and not a single tool between us that was actually designed for the job.

There is a difference between love and leverage. I had confused them for a long time. I thought if I loved her well enough, long enough, precisely enough... if I found the right words at the right moment... the scale would tip. The choice would become clear to her. The path out would open.

What I hadn't understood is that the path out was always open. It had been open for years. The question was never whether the path existed. The question was whether she was ready to walk it.

And she was not yet ready.

Staying would not make her ready. It would only give the fire more to consume.

Choosing my own life was not the end of the love. It was the most honest thing I could do with it.

. . .

The Ring

Dave found his limit not long after I found mine.

The shape of it was different than the way Rob's limit had arrived. Rob's had been a slow exhaustion… the quiet collapse of two people who had been trying in the same direction for so long that the effort had simply run out. What happened with Dave was sharper than that.

They were at a bar together one night. Ordinary enough on the surface. The kind of evening that doesn't announce itself as anything until it becomes everything.

She had been drinking. Not casually. The kind of drinking that takes you somewhere logic can't follow, where the inhibitions that keep us from doing the thing we shouldn't do simply… lower. And then disappear. She started paying attention to another man. Not quietly. Not with subtlety. She was hanging on him the way that happens when someone has crossed the line between where they meant to be and where the alcohol took them.

Dave watched it happen.

He was not a dramatic man. He didn't make a scene. He didn't erupt. He just... saw it. Clearly. With the particular clarity that arrives when you have been hoping for something long enough and you finally get a look at the truth underneath it. Not a misunderstanding. Not something that could be explained away in the morning. The plain truth of what he had been staying for and what it had cost him and what it was never going to become.

He left that night. Not in a rage. Just gone. The way decent people leave when they have finally understood that what they were hoping for is not on its way.

Some time after that, he showed me the ring.

I don't know why he showed me. Maybe because I was the one person in the situation who would understand exactly what it represented. Maybe because he needed someone to witness the weight of what he was holding. Maybe just because he needed to say it out loud to someone who had been inside the same fire and come out the other side of it.

It was an engagement ring. The one he had been carrying. The one that was supposed to be the beginning of the next chapter.

He held it in his hand and looked at it the way you look at something you intended to give but never got to. The weight of the unmade gesture. The future that had been planned for and prepared and then quietly cancelled by circumstances that had nothing to do with how much he had wanted it.

I didn't say much. There wasn't much to say.

What I felt, looking at that ring, was not just grief for him. It was a recognition. Another person who had come close. Who had stayed longer than most. Who had offered something real and specific and meant it with everything he had.

And the fire had taken it anyway.

That ring was not just a piece of jewelry. It was the tallied cost. The evidence of what untreated trauma actually does to the people who love the person carrying it. It moves from one to the next. Quietly, without announcement, without malice. It just keeps spreading. Rob. Dave. Me. All of us collateral damage in a war that had started long before any of us arrived.

I held it for a moment and handed it back.

He put it in his pocket and we didn't talk about it again.

. . .

The Difference Between Guilt and Grief

I have spent a long time learning to tell those two things apart.

They live in the same neighborhood. They have similar voices. They arrive at similar hours and they both feel like your fault. The confusion between them is one of the most expensive mistakes I know how to make, and I made it for years.

Guilt says: you caused this. You could have fixed it. You chose wrong. You left when you should have stayed. If you had just tried harder, been better, found the right words at the right moment... the outcome would have been different.

Grief says something else entirely.

Grief says: this was real. This mattered. The love was real and the loss is real and neither of those things cancels the other. You did not cause the wound. You could not close it. That is not a failure of your love. It is just the truth of what some wounds require.

The moment I grabbed her arm in that hallway and she went down... the question that arrived immediately after... am I becoming my father... that was guilt speaking. Trying to locate the damage in me. Trying to make the whole story about what I had done wrong instead of what the situation had been demanding for years.

It took me time to hear the grief underneath it. The real thing. The mourning of years of trying in a direction that was never going to work. The sadness of watching someone I loved choose the bottle over and over while I stood there holding everything I thought might help and watching none of it reach her.

Grief does not blame. It just witnesses.

It says: this happened. It cost something real. I did not deserve to carry it and neither did she and yet here we both were, inside it, doing the best we knew how with what we had.

Learning to grieve instead of guilt-spiral was not fast. It was not linear. It required the same kind of work that everything worth building requires... repetition, honesty, a willingness to sit with what is uncomfortable long enough to understand it instead of bury it.

But on the other side of that work is something worth having.

Not resolution. Not a clean conclusion. But a relationship to the past that doesn't keep making you pay for it in the present.

· · ·

The Bright Side

A line drawn in fire is still a line.

And the line I drew that night… the bag packed, the door closed, the decision made without a speech or a note or the permission of my guilt… that line was not the end of anything that mattered.

It was the beginning.

Not the dramatic kind of beginning. Not the kind that arrives with a sense of triumph or resolution or the clean feeling you imagine on the other side of a hard decision. The beginning was uncomfortable and uncertain and full of the particular grief that comes with choosing your own life when choosing your own life means watching someone else's cost continue to accumulate.

But it was still a beginning.

I moved into an apartment with people who were building something. I kept showing up to the school. I kept helping where I could, teaching what I knew, sitting at the edge of the mat on the days the injury flared and finding ways to be useful that didn't require me to be at full capacity. And in my early twenties, I bought into the school. What had started as a place I had come to as a broken kid looking for something to hold onto became, slowly and then all at once, something I had a stake in. Something I was building.

I was becoming someone.

Not in spite of everything that had happened. Not as an escape from it. Because of it. The years of watching. The years of carrying. The years of trying in directions that didn't work, of asking questions that didn't have easy answers, of holding things underground until the weight of them became something I had to reckon with honestly.

All of it was building something.

I understand that more clearly now than I could have then. The thing about purpose inside pain is that you almost never see it while you are inside the pain. You are too close to it. The image requires distance to resolve. You have to get far enough away from the burning building before you can see the shape of what it was trying to teach you.

Here is what the distance has shown me:

The boundary I drew that night was not selfish. It was stewardship. I rescued the only version of me that had any capacity to eventually be of use... to her, to the students I was teaching, to the wife I would one day commit myself to, to the children I would one day stand in front of and make a promise about who I intended to be for them.

You cannot pour from empty. You cannot lead from the bottom of a fire. You cannot build a legacy while everything you have is being poured into preventing a collapse that you do not have the tools to prevent.

Sometimes the most loving thing you can do is step back and let the truth land.

Sometimes the most courageous act available to you is the quiet one. Not the grand gesture. Not the dramatic intervention. Just the packed bag. Just the door. Just the decision to trust that your life is still worth protecting even when protecting it requires you to stop protecting someone who hasn't yet decided to protect themselves.

That is not cruelty. That is not giving up.

That is the hardest form of love there is. The kind that lets go. The kind that says: I cannot do this for you. But I will be here when you are ready. And in the meantime, I am going to become someone worth coming back to.

A line drawn in fire today may be the firewall that saves tomorrow's dreams.

Draw it.

Even when your hands are shaking.

Even when the guilt is loud.

Even when the grief of it doesn't resolve quickly.

Draw it anyway.

Because on the other side of that line is the version of your life that is still possible. Not the one you were handed. Not the one the storm tried to write for you. The one you are choosing. Right now. With everything you know and everything you've survived and everything you still intend to build.

That version is waiting.

Step toward it.

. . .

CHAPTER NINE

THE LIE OF UNWORTHINESS

I didn't plan on falling in love.

That probably sounds like a line. It isn't. It's just what happened.

By the time I was in my early twenties, I had built something. Not much, but something. A small martial arts school. Enough students to fill a mat. Enough income to keep the lights on and feed myself, if I didn't get too creative about what feeding myself meant. I was running something. Something that was mine.

It wasn't where I wanted to end up. It was where I was starting from. There's a difference, and I knew it.

What I didn't have yet was a clear picture of what a martial arts instructor could actually be. I had been taught technique. I had been taught discipline. What I hadn't been taught was how to reach someone. How to find the person inside the student and pull something forward in them that they didn't know was in there.

That part came from Dave McNeill.

. . .

The Architect

Dave McNeill is my instructor. And eventually, my dad.

Not by birth. By choice. Which, in my experience, is the kind that means more.

I've thought a lot about why Dave affected me the way he did. The simplest answer I can give is this: he didn't see martial arts as an end. He saw it as a tool. One of the best tools a person can have, but still a tool. The question he was always working from wasn't what can you do. It was what can this be used for.

He was an architect of improving lives. Not as a slogan. As a practice. You could see it in the way he taught, in the questions he asked, in the way he refused to be satisfied with technically correct when emotionally disengaged was sitting right next to it.

If my mother taught me that I have a choice... and that the fire inside a person can be aimed instead of just endured... then Dave taught me to dream about what that fire could build. Where I could be useful. What was possible if I stopped limiting the work to what was already familiar.

I absorbed all of it. I was hungry for it the way people are hungry when they've been surviving on something thin and finally sit down to a real meal.

It was Dave who put the Ultimate Black Belt Test in front of me.

. . .

The Test

Designed by Tom Callos, a martial arts coach and a genuine legend in that community, the Ultimate Black Belt Test was built to stretch the idea of what a black belt actually means. What it demands. What kind of person it's supposed to be building.

This wasn't a performance. It was a reckoning.

The physical requirements were serious and deliberate. 52,000 push-ups over the course of the program. Break it down and it's 150 a day. Manageable. The kind of number that sounds impossible until you do the math and realize it's just consistency, applied. 1,000 repetitions of a kata. Three reps a day. Show up. Do the work. Manage your body and your diet with the same intentionality you bring to the mat.

But the requirement that landed differently... the one that stopped me mid-sentence when I first heard it... wasn't a push-up count.

It was this: mend three broken relationships.

Not write about them. Not reflect on them from a comfortable distance. Go to them. Identify the places where your actions had broken something, and do the work to repair what could still be repaired.

I heard that requirement and I knew, before the words were fully out, exactly what it meant for me.

There was no deliberating. No list-making. No slow process of figuring out who qualified.

I was going to have to call my father.

I had known that was out there somewhere. The way you know a conversation is coming even when you've been successfully avoiding it for years. The weight of it had just been sitting in the background of my life, quiet enough to ignore on most days, heavy enough that I never quite forgot it was there.

The test had named it. And now I had to do something about it.

But first, there was Nevada.

. . .

Nevada, November

The test also required completing a reality-based self-defense course. There happened to be a Fast Defense training in Nevada in the middle of November 2006. Dave was on the team with us, along with his niece and a woman named Dani Carroll.

Our team was something. Highly qualified martial artists from different corners of the country, all serious about advancing not just in rank but in depth. The kind of people who understood that the belt is not the point. It's a marker. The work is the point.

I need to pause here and say something about Dave McNeill that only makes sense with a little distance: the man is efficient in the way a chess player is efficient. He doesn't force outcomes. He arranges conditions. He asks questions with obvious answers and lets you follow the logic to wherever he already knew it was going. He is, in the most affectionate possible way, a puppeteer... but not of manipulation. Of possibility.

Dave had formed a mentoring relationship with Dani. A guide, a friend, a person she trusted. And Dave, being Dave, had apparently decided at some point that she and I were going to find each other. He invited her to stay at his place for the training. Along with his niece. And me.

We all arrived in Nevada in November.

I saw Dani, and I immediately understood I was in some kind of trouble.

Not love at first sight. I want to be honest about that, because love at first sight belongs on greeting cards and this was something quieter than that. It was a curiosity. A pull. The particular attention you give something when your instincts have noticed it before your brain has caught up.

She was sharp. Warm in a way that didn't announce itself. Serious about her craft in the way I had learned to respect in people. A martial artist and a musician. Both at the same time, which told me something about the kind of depth she was carrying.

I watched her across the training and I thought, carefully: I need to pay attention to this person.

. . .

Every Night

After the training, we went back to our separate corners of the country. Me to Northeast Ohio. Dani to Middle Tennessee.

And then we started talking.

Every night. Nearly every night from November on. The kind of conversations that start with ordinary things and end up somewhere you didn't expect, in the best way. The kind of talking where you look up and two hours have disappeared and you're not entirely sure how you got from where you started to where you ended up, but you're glad you did.

With every conversation, the curiosity deepened. With every piece of information I collected about who she was, I became more interested. Not in the way you're interested in someone you're performing for. In the way you're interested when something real is happening and you know it and you're not sure what to do about it yet.

Dave noticed. Of course Dave noticed. Dave had probably noticed before either of us did.

He knew of a gym owner in Nashville who was looking to expand... to open additional schools and needed someone to build them. He also knew there were offers coming in for me from around the country. New Jersey. Atlanta. Boston. People who wanted someone to come in and build something for them.

Dave called me. He said, simply, there was a man in Nashville I should talk to. He thought it could be a good fit. Give him a call.

A week later I had a plane ticket.

The interview was in early December.

. . .

The First Date

The interview went well. They wanted to offer me the position.

But the first date with Dani was something different.

I had already told her I had feelings for her. She had responded in kind. But there is a meaningful distance between knowing something over the phone and standing in front of it. We went on that first date and something settled into place with a certainty I had never felt before and didn't entirely know what to do with.

I had thought the whole you just know thing was something people said after the fact to make the beginning feel fated. A story you tell once the ending is already written. I had no framework for it. It didn't fit with anything I had seen modeled about love or marriage growing up.

But that's what happened.

I knew.

Not the performance of knowing. Not the wishful version. The actual thing. The quiet, unmistakable, slightly terrifying thing. I looked at her and understood that this was the person I was going to spend my life with. Every reservation I had ever built up about marriage, every scar from watching what love could turn into, every whispered lie that told me I wasn't built for this kind of thing... it all went quiet.

I wanted to take care of her. I wanted to help her build her dreams. If for nothing else, just to watch her face when they came true.

I had been in relationships before. More than a few. And each one had followed its own version of the same arc. Proximity. Interest. Genuine connection, even. And then, at some point, the pieces wouldn't fit. I'd look at what we had and see the gap between it and what I actually needed, and I'd end up alone again.

I had poor examples of what a relationship was supposed to look like. I know that now. I carried that into every room without knowing I was carrying it. And beneath the not-knowing, there was something deeper...

a belief I had never examined out loud. Never put into words. Never held up to the light.

The belief that I was too damaged to be fully loved.

That the broken parts were too many and too deep. That anyone who got close enough to see all of it would eventually run the math and decide it didn't work in my favor.

My faith in marriage was somewhere near zero. I wasn't looking for a wife. I was just looking for someone to share the time with.

And then I was sitting across a table from Dani in Nashville, and everything I had decided about myself was losing ground.

. . .

April

We were engaged by April of 2007.

Fast, by most measurements. Certain, in a way that made the speed feel less like recklessness and more like clarity. When you know, you know. I had doubted that my whole life. I stopped doubting it sometime during that first date.

The wedding was planned for October. A quiet country wedding in the backyard of Dani's family home. Simple. Real. The kind of wedding that belongs to the people getting married and not to the production of it.

And then came the obvious question.

What about your parents?

Every engaged couple navigates the guest list. Who's coming. Who's sitting where. Who needs to know. It's logistical, until it isn't. For most people it's mildly complicated. For me, it opened a door I had been standing in front of for years without walking through.

I still had my aunt's number. She had called me years before to connect when my grandmother passed, and I had kept it in the way you keep certain things... not because you're sure you'll need them, but because something in you knows you might. I called her. Asked if she had my father's number.

She did.

Of course she did.

She gave it to me.

And then I did nothing with it for several days.

I want to be accurate about those days, because I think they matter. I wasn't frozen. I wasn't paralyzed in any dramatic way. I just kept looking at the number. It would sit there on my phone and I would pick it up and look at it and put it back down. There was no script for this conversation. No preparation that was going to make it less of what it was. It was just a phone number and a gap of years and everything that had happened in those years, sitting between me and a call I knew I needed to make.

The Ultimate Black Belt Test had asked me to mend broken relationships. Not think about it. Not intend to. Actually do it.

Eventually, I did.

. . .

The Call

The conversation was awkward at the start. Which is the only honest way to describe it. You don't skip years of silence and pick up smoothly. You feel your way through the beginning, both of you aware of the weight of what's sitting between you, neither of you quite sure how to set it down.

But it was healing.

That's the word I keep coming back to. Not resolved. Not finished. Healing. Like the first real breath after a long time of breathing shallow.

I told him I was getting married. That the wedding was in October. That I wanted him there.

And then I listened.

If you had known my father, you would know this about him: he had a laugh. A presence. He was funny in a way that could fill a room. He was capable of hiding the darker parts of himself behind a considerable amount of charm, but the one thing he was never able to hide was his joy. When something landed for him, when something genuinely delighted him, he would laugh in a way that was followed by whatever expletive his mood had selected for the occasion, and then he'd exhale, deeply, fully, the way a person exhales when they are completely and briefly content with the moment they're living in.

He laughed like that when I told him.

He congratulated me. He told me he was proud.

And then he said he was sorry he hadn't been around.

I don't know that I expected that. I don't know that I was prepared for it. There is something about receiving an apology you spent years not expecting that is its own particular kind of complicated. You don't always know what to do with it in the moment. You just receive it, and file it somewhere, and let time figure out what it means.

He said he'd be there in October.

And then he asked if he could call my mother. Whether they might be able to arrange to come down together.

I sat with that one for a minute.

My feelings about it were not simple. They never were when it came to the two of them in the same sentence. But I called my mother and told her what had happened. She agreed. I called him back with her number. And they began to talk again... after all those years, for the first time.

History does what it does. You can be surprised by it or you can observe it. I mostly just observed.

There's an irony in the wedding itself that is too specific to be coincidence, even if you're not someone who looks for those things. The wedding was in October. A quiet country ceremony in the backyard of Dani's family home. Intimate. Simple.

Which is exactly how my father and my mother were married... in the backyard of my grandparents' home, years before I existed.

He laughed about that too when I told him. That particular laugh. Expletive and all.

Some things just find each other.

. . .

October

The wedding was beautiful.

I couldn't have asked for anything more. Not a single thing. The kind of day that earns the word perfect not because nothing went wrong but because nothing that mattered went wrong, and the things that went right went so completely right that you stop keeping score.

And then there was the crowd.

If you had told me years earlier... the kid in that house, in that silence, measuring the temperature of every room before he walked into it... that he would one day stand at the front of a ceremony with three fathers present, I would not have believed you. I couldn't have even imagined it to disbelieve it.

But that's what happened.

My father was there. The man I had spent years trying to understand, then years trying to forget, then years working up the nerve to call. He was there.

My stepfather Rob was there. The man who had stepped into a situation that wasn't simple and had chosen to show up anyway. Who had given my mother and me something we hadn't had in a long time... stability. Presence. A version of family that held.

And Dave McNeill was there. My instructor. My mentor. The man who had taught me what it meant to use what you have to build something in someone else. The man I now call dad, not by birth but by everything that actually counts.

And then there was Dani's father. The man who had raised the woman walking toward me. Who had built the family that showed me, the first time I sat at their table, what a home was supposed to feel like. He didn't father me the way the others had. He did something different. He trusted me with his daughter. Which, when you think about it, is its own kind of choosing.

Four fathers. At my wedding.

I grew up believing I had been abandoned by the one I was supposed to have. And I stood in that backyard in Tennessee surrounded by four men who, each in their own way and in their own season, had chosen to father me.

The mothers were the same.

My momma was there. The woman who had lit a fire in me by surviving. Who had packed us up and walked us out and never stopped moving forward even when forward was hard to see.

Dani's mother was there. A woman with the kind of warmth that moves through a room quietly and makes everyone in it feel like they belong. She had welcomed me into her family without hesitation, and I had felt it from the first time I sat at their table.

And MaryAnn McNeill was there. Dave's wife. Who had extended the same warmth that Dave extended in his teaching, and made it clear that when Dave claimed you as family, she did too.

Three mothers.

I stood at the front of that ceremony and I looked at the woman walking toward me, and somewhere behind her I could see all of it. Everything it had taken to get to this exact moment. Every hard year. Every cracked place. Every conversation I had avoided and then finally had. Every person who had shown up in the gap when the people who were supposed to be there weren't.

And I thought, with complete clarity: I am the luckiest man alive.

I still think that. Most days with no reservations. Some days with a footnote about whether I deserve it.

Both of those things can be true at the same time.

. . .

What Was Still There

Underneath all of it, the trauma was still there.

I want to say that clearly, because I think it's important. Getting married didn't erase it. Finding the right person didn't erase it. What it did was give the trauma something to run up against. A presence that wouldn't confirm the lies.

After the wedding, Dani and I packed everything we owned and moved to Nevada. Not just her things. Everything we had, both of us, together. Because by then we were building one life, not two separate ones running parallel.

Dave McNeill lived in Nevada. I knew people there, at least some people. But knowing a handful of people and building a school from nothing in a new place are two different things. We built it from scratch. No existing students to inherit. No reputation already established. Just a mat, a lease, and the work of making something real out of nothing but belief and consistency.

Part of the arrangement was that Dani would fly back to Nashville every month to continue her music career. As newlyweds, I don't think I fully understood what I had agreed to when I said yes to that. Ten days out of every month, my wife was on a plane to Nashville while I was on a mat in Nevada, building something that didn't yet have the momentum to feel inevitable.

That was rough. I won't dress it up.

The absence poured gasoline onto every insecurity I had brought into the marriage without declaring it at the door. The fear of being left. The bone-deep certainty, installed in me long before I had words for it, that the people I loved would eventually go. That I was too much, or not enough, or some combination of both, and that the evidence would surface eventually and they would leave.

I had watched it happen enough times to believe it was just the pattern. My father, by violence and then by distance. My mother, by her own wounds and then literally. Relationships that got close and then didn't. The pattern was so consistent that I had stopped questioning whether it was going to repeat and started just waiting for when.

One night, the absence became too much.

The circumstances of that particular night pushed on every cracked place in me simultaneously. A massive argument. The kind of argument that lands you both on opposite sides of a room wondering if you made a mistake. If this was actually going to work. If you were even built for this.

I was being insecure. Untrusting. I felt unseen. I felt alone in the specific way that being alone inside a relationship feels worse than just being alone.

And then the temperature cooled.

And we talked.

And Dani looked at me and said something I wasn't expecting.

She didn't argue. She didn't defend herself. She didn't build a case or list everything she had done to prove she wasn't going anywhere.

She named it.

She said: I understand why you're afraid. Everyone you've ever loved has left you.

That was the whole sentence.

And something in me came loose.

I had carried that fear so long that it had become structural. I didn't know it was separate from me. I had just assumed it was the shape of things. The way they were always going to be. And she reached in and named it, quietly and without accusation, the way you name something that has been hiding in the dark and loses most of its power the moment someone turns on the light.

She said she was not going anywhere.

And I believed her.

That was almost nineteen years ago. She hasn't.

. . .

What Being Seen Actually Means

There is a difference between being fixed and being seen.

Dani didn't fix me. She didn't patch the scars. She traced them. She looked at the whole map of what I had been through and she honored the story beneath it instead of flinching at the edges.

Being fixed implies that something was wrong with you. Being seen implies that something was real about you. That the full weight of your history is not a defect to be corrected but a truth to be understood.

When I was finally able to drop the armor... when I stopped walking into rooms expecting something to go wrong, stopped waiting for the catch, stopped holding myself slightly apart from the people I loved as a hedge against the inevitable departure... I was finally able to see something I had been blocked from seeing.

My own value.

Not through my own assessment, which had been running off a faulty template for years. Through hers. Reflected back. As if she were holding up something I had never been able to see clearly in any mirror I had ever stood in front of.

Scarred does not mean damaged goods.

It means seasoned.

Every healed wound is testimony. Every scar is evidence not of what broke you but of what you survived. Resilient, not ruined. A witness, not a victim.

The lie of unworthiness is exactly that. A lie. It is what trauma whispers when it wants to keep you small. The voice that tells you the broken parts are too many, that anyone who sees the full picture will eventually walk away, that love is something that happens to other people who started with better raw material.

It is not true.

What is true is that the relationship that heals you... and it may be romantic, it may be platonic, it may be spiritual, it may be something that doesn't fit neatly into any category you have... begins with one thing.

Courageous exposure.

The willingness to show someone the cracks. To stop performing wholeness and let another person see the places that are still healing.

That is not weakness.

That is the bravest thing I know how to name.

The Ultimate Black Belt Test asked me to mend three broken relationships. I had sat with that requirement for months before I made the call. I had stared at a phone number and weighed the cost of what it might open up. I had made the call, had the awkward and healing conversation, had stood at a ceremony with both of my parents present at something that belonged to me.

I had not expected to also be mending the relationship with myself.

But that is what happened, slowly and without announcement, somewhere in the middle of all of it.

The test was designed to stretch what a black belt means. What kind of person earns one. What it demands beyond the physical.

Turns out it demanded this.

The courage to face what was broken. The willingness to reach toward something you weren't sure would reach back. The discipline to do the repair work even when you didn't know how it was going to go.

I didn't earn that belt by doing 52,000 push-ups.

I earned it by making the call.

· · ·

The Bright Side

I married way up. I say that with complete sincerity and only minor embarrassment.

There are days I don't feel like I deserve her at all. And then there are days when I think we deserve each other in a way that is too specific to be accidental. Both of those things are true at the same time. I've stopped trying to resolve the tension between them.

What I know is this: the version of me who believed he was too broken to be fully loved was wrong. Not because someone came along and fixed him. Because someone came along and refused to agree with the lie.

And in the space that opened up when the lie lost its grip... when someone finally named the fear and it stopped having the power to run my life from the shadows... I found out who I actually was.

Not a victim. Not damaged goods. Not someone whose early life had rendered him permanently unfit for connection.

A survivor. With scars. Who was capable of love and worthy of it.

The bright side of this particular brokenness is not that the pain wasn't real. It was. Not that the wounds didn't go deep. They did.

It's that the wounds didn't get the final word.

It's that the test that asked me to mend what was broken... externally, in the relationships I had let go dormant or damaged with my silence... ended up mending something internal that I hadn't even put on the list.

It's that a quiet country wedding in a backyard in Tennessee, with both parents present and a woman beside me who had refused to confirm my worst beliefs about myself, was not the ending of anything.

It was the beginning of everything.

You don't have to be unbroken to be loved. You just have to be brave enough to let someone see what you are.

. . .

CHAPTER TEN

THE WHOLE POINT

. . .

There is a moment that lives in my chest like a second heartbeat.

I'm standing in a hospital room. The lights are the kind that hum. The air smells like antiseptic and something almost sacred. And in my arms, for the first time, is my son.

He was not small. I want to be clear about that. The nurses had opinions about him from the moment he arrived. They called him Tank ... affectionately, but accurately. He came into the world with a full head of hair and an energy that announced itself, and the nurses had swept that hair into a little fo-hawk that made him look like he already had somewhere important to be.

That was my boy. Big and bold and already himself.

But before I held him, I watched his mother.

I watched Dani fight for him the way only a mother fights. That particular kind of relentless, all-in, nothing-held-back effort that has no ego in it ... it is just pure love translated into will. And standing there in that room, watching her, something clicked into place that I hadn't fully seen before.

She was going to fight for him the way my mother had fought for me.

That is not a small thing to witness. I had grown up watching my mother absorb things that would have broken most people, and keep moving anyway, because she had a child to protect. I knew what that looked like. I knew what it cost. And now here was Dani, doing the same thing, for the same reason ... and I understood in that moment that my son was going to have what I had always needed most.

Someone who would not stop fighting for him.

And then the nurse placed him in my arms. Full head of hair. Fo-hawk and everything. And I am looking at this person who has done nothing, earned nothing, inherited nothing yet ... and the weight of that word hits me all at once.

Yet.

Because here is the truth I was sitting with in that moment: I knew exactly what could be passed down. I had lived it. I had worn it. I had carried it through years that cost me more than I could have calculated at the time. And now this child ... my child ... was standing at the beginning of a story, and I was the one who would write the first chapters.

That is a weight I didn't know existed until I felt it.

And right there, in that room, with that big healthy boy in my arms and his mother's strength still hanging in the air, I made a decision.

Not a wish. Not a hope. A decision.

The cycle stops here.

. . .

What the Broken Man Builds

I want to be honest with you about something before we go any further.

I did not arrive at this chapter as a polished man with all the answers. I arrived here the way most people arrive at anything real ... slowly, imperfectly, and with a few scars that still ache when the weather changes.

Everything in the chapters before this one was the ground being broken. The childhood in a home filled with violence and fear. The Necco Wafers. The living room at night with the TV glow and my mother's eyes. The night we finally left. The years that followed where the leaving didn't cure everything, because leaving never does. The borrowed beliefs, the borrowed confidence, the borrowed sense of self that I had to borrow from people willing to lend it until I could build my own. The return of my father. The boundaries that had to be drawn in fire. The scars that Dani loved through when she had every right to walk away.

All of that happened. It is real. I am not asking you to soften it or skip over it.

But now I want to tell you what it was for.

Because I believe it was for something.

I believe that with everything I am.

. . .

The Book on the Table

There's a moment from earlier in this story ... Dave, my mother's boyfriend, a kitchen table covered in components, a technical manual, and a smirk.

Have at it, young man.

That book knew everything. Every connection. Every failure point. Every reason a system could break down and exactly why. It didn't know those things because someone sat in a classroom and studied theory. It knew them because someone had lived through every mistake first. Had built things wrong, watched them fail, figured out what went wrong and why, and written it all down so the next person wouldn't have to start from zero.

That knowledge was earned. By experience. By failure. By getting it wrong enough times to finally understand how to get it right.

And because of that, it was the most valuable thing on the table.

You are building that book.

Every hard year. Every wound you carried that you didn't ask for. Every time you had to figure out how to survive something that had no instructions. It is all being written. Not on a shelf somewhere. On you. In you. In the specific, unduplicatable way that only lived experience can write.

Someone who grew up safe cannot tell you what it feels like to measure the temperature of a room before you walk into it. They can read about it. They can empathize with it. But they cannot say, from the inside, 'I know exactly what that is.'

You can.

That is not a wound. That is a credential.

And once you stop carrying it like a burden and start recognizing it for what it is ... you become exactly what someone else needs. Someone who has been inside the thing. Someone who knows every failure point. Someone who can say, with complete authority, 'I know how this breaks. And I know how to build it better.'

That is the whole point.

. . .

Grateful for All of It

I had to wrestle with something for a long time before I could write this chapter.

The question was this: how do you hold gratitude for things that hurt you?

Because the easy answer is that you don't. The easy answer is that gratitude is for the good things, the blessings, the moments where the light came through. And I understand why people stop there. It's safer there. Gratitude for the good is clean. Gratitude for the bad is complicated.

But here is what I have learned, and what I believe now with a clarity that took decades to build:

If you are going to be grateful for the blessings in your life ... truly grateful, down to the bone ... you have to also be grateful for the hard things.

Not in a way that minimizes them.

Not in a way that pretends they didn't cost you.

But in a way that acknowledges this truth: the person you are today was built by all of it. The gentle things and the brutal things. The moments of grace and the moments of chaos. The Necco Wafers and the nights when the TV was the only safe light in the room.

You cannot selectively accept the shaping.

The same fire that destroyed some things in you also forged the parts you now stand on.

The empathy I carry for people who were raised in chaos ... that didn't come from nowhere. It came from knowing chaos. The instinct I have to protect children and show them they are safe ... that didn't come from a textbook. It came from being a child who needed protecting and didn't always have it.

The patience. The awareness. The ability to recognize a hurt person walking in the door of my life before they've said a word ... all of it was built in the hard years.

Broken does not mean useless.

Broken means experienced. Broken means educated in a way that comfort could never teach. Broken means you now carry knowledge that someone, somewhere, desperately needs.

. . .

My Son. My Daughter. My Decision.

When my son was born, the decision was clear but the work was still ahead of me.

I decided that what my father had modeled for me would not be what I modeled for him. I decided that the cycle ... the pattern that had been running through my family like a current I didn't ask to be born into ... would stop with me. That he would know what it felt like to have a father who showed up. A father who stayed. A father whose presence in the room meant safety, not the absence of it.

I wanted him to grow up never having to wonder.

Never having to calculate whether the mood in the house was safe tonight.

Never having to earn the love that should have just been there.

And then we had our daughter.

And the decision deepened in a different direction.

With her, I thought about her mother.

Dani ... my wife, my partner, the woman who loved me through the years when I was still assembling the person I was trying to become ... she is one of the strongest human beings I have ever known. Her strength is not loud. It's steady. It's the kind of strength that shows up at 2 a.m. and doesn't complain about it. The kind that holds things together while quietly refusing to be diminished.

I want my daughter to have that strength.

I want her to see what it looks like. Not just in her mother ... but in how her mother is treated. Because daughters learn what they deserve from watching how the women in their lives are valued.

I want her to look at the way I love Dani and know, at a cellular level, the standard she should carry into every relationship she ever chooses.

I want her to never accept less than what she watches us build every day.

That is what we are modeling. Every dinner together. Every conversation where we disagree and work it through instead of exploding. Every moment where she sees her parents choose each other, deliberately, on an ordinary Tuesday.

Those moments are curriculum.

They are writing a story in her that she will carry for the rest of her life.

. . .

Family First. Always.

Our martial arts schools are called Family First Martial Arts.

That is not just a name. It is a declaration.

When I look at what I wanted to build in my life, it was never primarily a business. It was a place where children learn that they are capable. Where they develop the discipline that becomes confidence, and the confidence that becomes identity, and the identity that carries them through every hard thing life puts in front of them.

It was a place where the values I had to learn the hard way could be taught in an environment that felt safe.

Where fathers show up and see their kids earn something.

Where families sit in the same room and cheer for each other.

Where a child who has never been told they are strong begins to believe it ... not because we told them, but because they proved it to themselves.

The name Family First came from the center of everything I believe. Not because families are perfect. Not because the families who walk through our doors haven't had their own hard chapters. But because the family unit, when it is healthy, when it is committed, when it is protected and prioritized ... is the most powerful force for healing and formation in a human life.

I know what it costs when it's absent.

I know what it gives when it's present.

I have lived both sides of that truth, and I am telling you: the presence matters more than words can hold.

So we built something that puts it first. In our home. In our business. In how we raise our kids and how we love each other and how we show up for the people who come to us for help.

Family First is not a slogan.

It is the answer to everything I didn't have growing up.

. . .

What Healing Actually Looks Like

People talk about healing like it is a destination.

Like one day you arrive somewhere, plant a flag, and say: 'I'm done. I'm healed. The work is finished.'

That is not how it works.

Healing is not a place you reach. It's a direction you keep choosing.

I still have moments. Moments where something triggers the old wiring ... a tone of voice, a certain kind of tension in a room, a situation that rhymes with something from decades ago ... and I feel it. Not as loudly as I once did. Not with the same grip. But I feel it.

The difference is what I do with it now.

Early on, I didn't have tools. I navigated by instinct and stubbornness and a deep refusal to become what I had seen. That got me through. But it wasn't the same as healing. It was surviving with a clear direction.

Healing came through Dani. Through the safety of being truly known by someone who wasn't going anywhere. Through the hard work of learning to receive love without waiting for it to become something else. Through being a father and discovering that the parts of me I was most afraid of ... the parts that worried me in quiet moments ... were not inevitable. They were patterns. And patterns can be interrupted.

I interrupted them.

Not perfectly. Never perfectly.

But consistently. Intentionally. With the kind of deliberate effort that doesn't make for dramatic stories but is, in fact, the actual work of becoming someone different than what you inherited.

That is available to you too.

Not as a promise that it will be easy. It won't be.

But as a truth I have lived: the patterns that were handed to you are not locked inside you. They are running. And running things can be stopped.

. . .

Pain Has a Purpose

I have thought a long time about why God let me go through every detail of what you've read in these pages.

The fear in that trailer. The confusion of a child trying to understand violence in the one place that was supposed to be safe. The years my mother fought and struggled and sometimes lost. The complicated grief of loving a father who was also the source of the wound. The years of building myself from borrowed pieces until I found the solid ground of knowing who I was and what I was for.

I have thought about why all of it.

And the answer I have arrived at is not complicated, even though it took a long time to reach:

It was so I could help others through it.

Not despite what happened. Because of it.

The specificity matters. The details matter. When someone sits across from me and tells me about a childhood they couldn't control, I don't nod politely from a distance. I recognize it. I know the particular kind of quiet that falls over a room when the wrong person comes home. I know what it costs a child to stay small and still and invisible. I know the way you love someone who also frightens you ... how those two things live together in the same chest without canceling each other out.

I know that because I lived it.

And that knowledge ... that costly, hard-earned, scar-tested knowledge ... is exactly what makes it possible for me to reach someone that a smoother life couldn't touch.

You cannot fake your way into that kind of connection.

You can only earn it.

I earned it the only way it can be earned.

And I do not say that with bitterness. I say it with something that took me a long time to get to but that I now hold without apology:

Gratitude.

For all of it. The beautiful and the brutal. The gifts and the wounds.

Because they made me someone who can stand in front of a broken person and say, with complete honesty, 'I have been here. And there is a way through.'

. . .

Rising from the Ashes

There are people reading this right now who are still inside the hard chapter.

Who have not yet found the door.

Who are carrying things they haven't told anyone, because they learned early that telling people cost more than keeping it.

I want to speak directly to you for a moment.

You are not defined by what was done to you.

I know you've heard that before. I know it can sound like a line. But it is true in the most practical, concrete, livable sense: the story of your life is not finished, and the chapters that have already been written do not have the final word about what gets written next.

Broken does not mean done.

Broken means you have knowledge. Experience. Scar tissue that is, medically speaking, stronger than the original. The things that tried to destroy you did not succeed ... they equipped you.

They gave you a language that comfort cannot speak.

They gave you a credential that no classroom offers.

They gave you the capacity to reach the people that polished presentations and easy lives cannot reach.

If you are strong enough to rise ... and I believe you are, because you are still here, still reading, still reaching for something better ... then your ashes are not the end of the story.

They are the material.

They are what you build from.

And what you build from them ... the family you protect, the children you raise differently, the people you guide through what you already survived ... that is the bright side.

Not a consolation prize.

A purpose.

The whole, actual, hard-won, God-given purpose of everything you went through.

. . .

The Bright Side of Brokenness

This is what the title was always pointing toward.

Not the idea that bad things are secretly good.

Not the suggestion that you should be grateful for abuse or loss or years stolen from you.

But this:

The same experiences that broke something in you also built something in you. Both are true. You do not have to choose which one to believe. You hold both ... and you let the building matter as much as the breaking.

The person you are today was assembled from everything. The love and the fear. The kindness you received and the cruelty you survived. The people who saw you and the people who failed you. The moments of grace and the long stretches of just getting through.

All of it is in you.

All of it is you.

And all of it ... when you stop being at war with your own history ... becomes a resource.

My son will grow up knowing what a present father looks like. My daughter will grow up knowing what a valued woman looks like. The children who walk through the doors of Family First Martial Arts will learn discipline in an environment of safety. The people who read these pages will know they are not alone.

That is what it was all for.

Every hard night. Every piece of fear. Every moment I had to decide what kind of man I was going to be. Every borrowed belief that carried me until I could build my own. Every conversation with Dani where I had to choose to stay open instead of shutting down. Every time I stood in front of a room full of kids and thought about the child I once was and what he needed.

All of it was building toward this.

The only thing left is to be brave enough to give it away.

To open the book.

To turn to the page where someone else needs help.

And to say, without hesitation:

I know this chapter. I've read it before. Let me show you what I found on the other side.

. . .

The Bright Side

Broken does not mean useless. It means experienced.

Every wound that didn't finish you has been quietly converting itself into wisdom. The hard parts of your story are not evidence of failure. They are curriculum. Hard-won, personally paid for, and more valuable than anything that came easy.

If you are grateful for the blessings in your life ... and I believe you are ... then consider extending that gratitude further. To the hard years too. Not because they were good, but because they made you capable. Because they gave you something to offer. Because the people who need you most will not need your polished parts. They will need the parts that understand what it is to struggle.

The cycle you refuse to pass down becomes a gift to people who haven't been born yet.

The home you build with intention becomes proof, to your children, that something different is possible.

The voice you find ... the voice that says 'I have been here and there is a way through' ... is the most important voice in the room for the person standing where you once stood.

That is the bright side.

Not that the pain was worth it in some tidy, transactional sense.

But that the pain was not wasted.

That it was always, even when it didn't feel like it, building something.

And that something ... is you.

. . .

CHAPTER ELEVEN

WHAT FORGIVENESS ACTUALLY COSTS

...

I had played it out in my mind before.

Not often. Not deliberately. Just every now and then, in the quiet between things, the thought would arrive uninvited and I'd let it run for a moment before I moved it along. A fleeting thing. The kind of practice scenario the mind runs without asking your permission.

I wondered what I would do when the call came.

How I would take it. Whether I would feel anything. Whether the years of distance and silence and careful management had done what part of me had privately hoped they would ... built enough space between me and him that the news, when it finally arrived, would land somewhere I didn't have to feel it.

I thought I was ready.

...

The Call

It was my uncle's voice that told me something was wrong before his words did.

There is a particular quality to a voice that is carrying something heavy. You know it before you know what it's carrying. The way your name lands differently. The pause before the first sentence that isn't quite long enough to explain but is long enough to prepare you for the fact that preparation won't help.

I heard it immediately.

And then he told me.

I already knew about the cancer. That part wasn't new. My father had been diagnosed, and the news from the doctors had been cautiously encouraging ... treatment was likely going to work. It wasn't the ending anyone was preparing for. It was the kind of diagnosis you process as a detour, not a destination. You adjust. You wait. You let the medicine do what medicine is supposed to do.

My uncle said, "Larry ... your father is gone."

I went to my knees.

He hadn't told me how yet. Just those five words. And they were enough to take me down.

Then he told me how.

My father had gone out to his backyard. And he had made the last decision himself.

What I remember most about that moment ... beyond the floor, beyond what was coming out of me ... was the confusion. Not about what had happened. About myself. About my own response.

I had thought about this before. Not obsessively, but the thought had crossed my mind the way certain thoughts do ... quietly, without invitation. What will I feel when he's gone. And when I had run that scenario, the answer that came back felt honest. I thought I would be sad. The way I was sad when his mother passed. That news had landed ... a genuine sorrow, a recognition of loss. But I wasn't rocked. I processed it and I kept moving.

I expected this to be like that.

I was wrong.

My legs gave out at five words. Before I even knew how. And what came out of me was something I had never heard from myself before. Not grief in any form I recognized. Something beneath grief. Something that had been stored in a place I had convinced myself, for years, was sealed.

I sobbed the way a child sobs.

The kind that doesn't care who hears it. That bypasses every layer of composure you've built over decades and goes straight to the thing underneath. The thing that existed before the work and the discipline and the boundaries and the chosen family. Before all of it.

The boy at the crib rail, waiting to hear if his mother was still there.

That's who went to his knees.

And the gap between who I thought I would be in that moment and who I actually was ... that gap told me something I hadn't fully known until the floor came up to meet me.

I loved him.

Through all of it. In spite of all of it. Underneath all of it.

I loved my father.

And I had never let myself know how much until the moment he was gone.

. . .

What I Realized in the Grief

I had expected, if I was honest with myself, a version of relief. Not satisfaction ... I was not that person. But the complicated release that comes when something you have been bracing against for years finally resolves. The chapter that was always going to end badly, ending.

What I did not expect was what I found underneath the grief.

Forgiveness.

Not decided. Not worked toward through some deliberate process of reflection and release. Discovered. Already there. The way you discover something that has been in the room the whole time, that you just couldn't see until the light changed.

All of the anger ... the kind I had managed for so long I had started to mistake it for a permanent feature of who I was ... was gone. The resentment that had lived underneath the work and the discipline and the careful construction of a life I was proud of. The banked heat of what had been done and what had never been properly answered for.

Gone.

What was left was grief. Real grief. Not for the father I'd had, but for the father that was never going to exist now. For the relationship that wasn't going to happen. Not because the door was closed ... but because the man was gone.

You can't reconcile with a grave.

That is its own particular kind of loss. And it deserves to be named as one.

. . .

A Month in His House

I went to take care of his affairs.

My aunts were there. We spent nearly a month together, the three of us, picking up the pieces of his life and our shattered hearts at the same time. The kind of work that is practical and devastating in equal measure ... sorting through the accumulated evidence of a life, deciding what matters and what doesn't, making a hundred small decisions while carrying something too large for small decisions to contain.

I don't know what I expected to find.

What I found was a man.

Not the monster I had built in my head during the worst years. Not the diminished stranger I had confronted during the UBBT. A man. With the particular texture and weight of a human being who had occupied space in the world for decades and left evidence of it behind.

When you have to go through everything a person kept hidden in their closets ... you learn who they actually were.

I saw the mental illness. Not suspected, not inferred. Present. Documented in the things he'd kept and the things he hadn't thrown away. A mind that had been at war with itself for longer than I had been alive.

I saw the generational damage. Evidence of what had been done to him, and to his siblings, before he ever did anything to anyone else. His father. The same patterns. The same wounds. The same cycle playing out one generation back, and probably further than that.

I understood, standing in that house, that my father was not the beginning of this story. He was somewhere in the middle of it. Shaped by things that were done to him before I was born, handed a way of being in the world that was already broken before he ever broke anything himself.

And then I saw what he had done with it.

He had shoved it down.

All of it. Everything that needed to be named and looked at and worked through ... he had pushed it below the surface and he had kept pushing. And the things you push down don't disappear. They find another way out. They start coming sideways. In the violence. In the drinking. In the way a man can be in a room full of people who love him and still be completely unreachable.

He had shoved it all down until there was nowhere left for it to go.

. . .

What His Hands Could Do

Here is the thing that broke me open in a different way.

My father was a craftsman.

Not casually. Not as a hobby. The man could build things that stopped people in their tracks. Works of art made from raw material and a set of worn-down tools and a vision in his head that his hands knew exactly how to bring into the world. You could see it everywhere in that house. The details that didn't have to be there but were. The care in things that no one would notice unless they knew to look. The evidence of a mind that saw possibility in a piece of wood the way other people see it on a finished shelf.

I stood in rooms he had built and I was genuinely moved.

And then the irony of it landed on me and I couldn't shake it.

This man ... who could take a vision that existed only in his mind and make it real with a few worn-down tools ... this man could not build the life he deserved. He had the hands for it. He had the vision for it. He had, underneath everything, the capacity for something extraordinary.

But he couldn't build that.

He never figured out how.

And I believe ... I have to believe, because the alternative is too bleak to sit inside for long ... that he deserved a good life. Not because of what he did. In spite of it. Because every person, underneath the damage and the choices and the patterns they were handed and the ones they chose to keep, deserves the chance at something better.

He just never gave himself that chance.

And that is a tragedy I will carry quietly for the rest of my life.

. . .

What I Remembered

I stood in his house for a month and I let the memories come.

All of them. Not just the ones I had been carrying. The ones I had filed away or forgotten or not allowed myself to return to because the surrounding context made them feel dangerous.

I honored the bad memories. They are real and they happened and they deserve their space in the record.

But there were good ones too.

Our wedding. He was there. And I remember watching him in that room ... relaxed, happy, with no weather coming off of him, just a man genuinely glad to be present for something good. We had come far enough from the beginning that we could stand in the same room and feel something other than damage between us. That was not a small thing to have.

And the phone call when I told him he was going to be a grandfather.

I can still hear his voice in that moment. The way the news hit him. Pure joy ... the unguarded, unmanaged, immediate kind that bypasses whatever a person has built around themselves and just arrives on the surface. He was elated. Absolutely lit up by it. And when he found out it was going to be a granddaughter ... something in him that I hadn't heard before. Something tender and enormous at the same time.

That laugh.

God, I miss that laugh.

It was specific to him in a way that is hard to describe ... big and sudden and completely unself-conscious, the kind of laugh that made you want to be the reason for it. And when he laughed for his granddaughter who hadn't arrived yet, it was the most alive I had ever heard him.

I wish there had been more time. More of those moments. More chances for her to know the good parts of him. For him to know her. To watch her grow into whoever she is going to be. To hear her laugh back.

Those are the things his choice took from all of us.

I grieve those too.

. . .

His Tools

I have his tools now.

They sit in my space the way his hands once moved through his. Worn down in the right places. Carrying the particular weight of something that has been used for real work over a long time.

I build things too. Not the works of art he built. Nothing that would stop people in their tracks or make them wonder how it was done. Just things. Shelves. Repairs. The ordinary constructions of an ordinary life.

But what I choose to build with the tools I possess ... are kids.

Most of them come to Family First Martial Arts for entirely good reasons. They want to learn something cool. They want the confidence that comes from knowing how to handle themselves. They want better focus, better discipline, a place where they are expected to rise to something and given the tools to do it. Parents bring them because they see potential that needs direction. Because they want their child to know what they're made of before the world gets a chance to tell them otherwise.

That is the ordinary, beautiful work of the mat. And I love that work. Every kid who walks out of that building standing a little taller than when they walked in ... every parent who watches something click into place in their child that they couldn't manufacture at home ... that is the reason I built what I built. That is enough. That has always been enough.

But every once in a while ...

Every once in a while, I see myself walk through those doors.

Not literally. But I know what I'm looking at. The way they check the room before they fully enter it. The stillness that isn't shyness ... it's something older than shyness. The particular quality of a child who has learned to measure the atmosphere before committing to a space. Who has been reading rooms since before they had words for why.

I know that child. I was that child.

And those kids need me in a way that is different from the others. Not more important ... every child in that building matters completely. But different. Because what they need isn't just a skill or a belt or a better report card. What they need is someone who sees them. Who knows what they're carrying without being told. Who can stand in front of them and be living proof that the thing they're surviving right now is not the final word on who they are going to become.

I can be that for them. Because someone was that for me.

Rob. Dave. My mother's refusal to stop fighting. Every person who handed me a borrowed belief when I had none of my own.

The mat is where I pay that forward. With whatever I have. With tools worn down in the right places. Toward something that lasts.

Toward something worth building.

. . .

What This Is Not

I want to be careful here. Because there is a version of this chapter that uses what I found in his life as softening. As a way of arriving at something that sounds like an excuse.

That is not what this is.

My father had mental illness. Real and documented and consequential. He lived in an era and a culture and a family that gave him no language for it and no acceptable path to help.

My father carried generational damage. He was not the beginning of the pattern. He was somewhere in the middle of it, handed a broken way of being before he ever broke anything himself.

All of that is true.

None of it absolves him.

Because at some point, every person who has been handed damage stands at a crossroads. The road they were given. And the road they could choose.

He stood at that crossroads more than once. More than I will ever know.

And he kept going the same direction.

He didn't learn the lessons. He didn't choose the harder path. He didn't do the work. He took what he inherited and he passed it forward instead of stopping it cold.

That was a choice. Whatever was underneath it ... the illness, the damage, the absence of any map to something better ... the choice was still a choice.

And it cost him everything.

His marriage. His son. His granddaughter, who carries his laugh in her face without knowing it. The last years of his life. The version of himself that might have been, if he had picked up the other set of tools.

I don't say that with satisfaction. I say it because it's the most important thing I can give someone reading this who is still standing at that crossroads.

The road you're on has a destination.

So does the other one.

You still get to choose.

. . .

What Forgiveness Is

I spent years misunderstanding forgiveness. I thought it meant reconciliation. That you couldn't say you forgave someone without also saying what they did was acceptable. As if the debt were being cancelled.

It isn't that.

Forgiveness is not a verdict. It's not an agreement that what happened didn't matter or that the cost wasn't real. Forgiveness is a release. The decision to stop carrying someone else's debt in your own body. Not for their sake … for yours. Because the anger doesn't punish the person who caused it. It lives in you. It occupies space. It shapes how you move through rooms and relationships and quiet moments that were never supposed to be about him at all.

I didn't forgive my father because he deserved it.

I forgave him because I was done letting what he chose define what I carried.

The grief that came with his death was real. And underneath all of it … the love. The stubborn, irrational, unkillable love that a child has for a parent, that persists even when everything in the record argues against it. Grief and love and anger and confusion and relief, all at once, all on the floor of wherever I was when the call came.

That is what forgiveness actually costs. Not the easy decision. The willingness to grieve someone who hurt you. To feel the love that was always there underneath the damage. To let both things be true at the same time without asking either one to cancel the other.

I sobbed for the father I had.

And for the one I never got to have.

Both of those men deserved to be grieved.

. . .

The Bright Side

He built beautiful things.

And he couldn't build the life he deserved.

I think about that. A lot.

The gap between what a person is capable of creating and what they actually build with their life ... that gap is not a mystery. It is a choice. Made over and over, in small moments and large ones, in what you decide to face and what you decide to shove down.

His worn-down tools sit in my space now.

I don't build what he built. I build differently. With different materials. Toward a different vision.

But I think he would understand, if he could see it. The way you can recognize the same instinct in a different form. The need to take something raw and make it into something that matters. To bring a vision out of your head and into the world and have it be real and lasting and worth the effort.

I think that is who he was, underneath everything. Someone who wanted to build things that lasted.

He just never found the right materials.

I have his tools.

And I know what to build with them.

Most days, the building looks ordinary. A kid who learns to focus. A kid who learns to fall and get back up. A kid who earns something through effort and discovers they are capable of more than they knew.

That work is enough. That work is everything.

But every once in a while, I see myself walk through those doors.

And those kids …

those kids need what I have.

Not my credentials. Not my technique.

My story.

That is the bright side.

Not that the pain was worth it in some tidy sense.

But that the pain became material.

He built with wood.

I build with people.

And what I build … will outlast both of us.

. . .

Support
Resources

If You Need Help ... Here Is Where to Start

My mother did not have this list. The infrastructure for it barely existed in her era, and what did exist came wrapped in enough stigma that reaching for it felt like a risk she couldn't afford.

You have it. Right now. In your hand or on your screen.

These are real resources. Free, confidential, and staffed by people who are not there to judge you ... only to help you find the next right step. You do not have to have it figured out before you call. You do not have to know exactly what you need. You just have to make the call.

If you or someone you love is struggling with alcohol, addiction, or the kind of untreated pain that drives both ... start here.

SAMHSA National Helpline | 1-800-662-4357 | samhsa.gov

Free, confidential, 24/7. English and Spanish. Substance use and mental health referrals for individuals and families. Text your ZIP code to 435748 to find local resources.

988 Suicide & Crisis Lifeline | Call or text 988

For anyone in emotional distress or crisis. Not only for suicide ... if the weight is too heavy right now, this line is for you.

Crisis Text Line | Text HOME to 741741

Free, 24/7. If calling feels like too much right now, texting is enough. A trained crisis counselor will be on the other end.

Al-Anon / Alateen | 1-800-356-9996 | al-anon.org

For the people who love someone struggling with alcohol. If you grew up in a home like mine, or if someone you love is in one right now ... this line exists for you, not just for them.

NAMI Helpline | 1-800-950-6264 | nami.org

National Alliance on Mental Illness. Peer support, practical resources, and next steps for people living with mental health conditions and their families.

FindTreatment.gov | findtreatment.gov

SAMHSA's treatment locator. Enter your location and find nearby facilities, programs, and providers.

National Association for Children of Alcoholics | 1-888-554-2627

If you grew up in a home shaped by a parent's drinking and you are still carrying the weight of those years ... this line exists for you specifically.

These numbers exist because the people who built them understand something essential: asking for help is not the end of your story. It is where the better part of it begins.

The answers are never at the bottom of a bottle. But they are at the other end of a phone call.

ABOUT THE AUTHOR

Larry Kooyman is a husband, father, martial arts school owner, leadership developer, and ... someone who has learned that the building never really stops.

He spent decades building things ... businesses, systems, relationships, a reputation ... only to discover that the most important building happens on the inside. The Bright Side of Brokenness is his honest account of that discovery.

Larry and his wife are the co-founders of Family First Martial Arts, where for over two decades they have trained students not just in technique, but in character. Their schools are built around a driving personal value: every child who walks through the door deserves to be seen, challenged, and believed in. He also consults martial arts school owners across the country to make lasting positive change in their communities.

Before any of that, he was a kid who grew up inside a storm he did not create. This book is the story of what that storm deposited in him ... and what he fought to build from it.

He is a coach, a speaker, and occasionally ... a guy who gets things completely wrong and has to find his way back.

That last part, he'll tell you, is where the best lessons live.

Larry lives a blessed life with his wife and family, striving to do good in the world. When he's not on the mat or behind a whiteboard, you'll find him searching for the courage to keep telling the truth.

. . .

Connect with Larry

Book website:
brightsideofbrokenness.com

Author website:
larrykooyman.com

To purchase signed copies of this book for your event, visit:
brightsideofbrokenness.com

To book Larry to speak at your event, visit:
larrykooyman.com

BRING LARRY TO YOUR EVENT

Most people spend their lives hiding the broken pieces.

Tucking them away. Editing them out. Presenting the version of themselves that looks like they have it together ... while carrying the weight of everything they've never said out loud.

Larry Kooyman believes those broken pieces are not the problem. They are the point. Every crack. Every scar. They did not diminish your light. They are how it gets out.

Larry speaks to churches, ministries, and men's groups who are ready to go beneath the surface. His talks are built on lived experience, hard-won clarity, and the kind of honesty that makes people feel safe enough to tell the truth about where they actually are. He doesn't speak at people. He speaks with them ... meeting them where they are and helping them find what's still possible from right there.

People don't leave his talks motivated. They leave seen.

. . .

Larry is available for:

- Churches and ministry events

- Men's groups and men's conferences

- Keynotes and conference sessions

- Leadership retreats and team development

- Youth and family events

- Podcast and media interviews

Speaking Topics Include:

- The Bright Side of Brokenness ... Turning Pain into Purpose

- Breaking the Chain ... How Generational Patterns End with You

- Building People First ... Leadership That Starts from the Inside Out

- The Vow You Made Before You Had Words for It ... Identity, Fatherhood, and Choosing Different

- Branding ... The Value in Telling Your Story ... Why Authenticity Is Your Greatest Competitive Advantage

If you have been carrying something heavy and need to know you are not alone ... this message is for you.

If you lead a room full of people who need to hear that their broken pieces are not wounds but gifts ... Larry would love to bring this message to them.

. . .

To book Larry for your next event, visit:
larrykooyman.com

Signed and bulk copies of this book are available for your event at:
brightsideofbrokenness.com

The courage to tell the truth changes rooms.

Larry has done it in this book.

He'd love to do it in yours.